This cover photograph shows Peter Craven in a characteristic action pose.

Speedway Panorama

Speedway Panorama

by Ron Hoare

ISBN 0 85429 252 7

© Ron Hoare 1979

First published March 1979

A FOULIS Motorcycling Book

Printed and bound in England by the publishers:
Haynes Publishing Group
Sparkford, Yeovil, Somerset BA22 7JJ, England

Distributed in North America by:
Haynes Publications Inc
861 Lawrence Drive, Newbury Park, California 91320, USA

Editor: **Jeff Clew**
Cover design: **Phill Jennings**
Layout design: **Rowland Smith**

Contents

Foreword

Introduction

1 Down memory lane with Johnnie Hoskins

2 Birthplace of British dirt track racing

3 Golden Anniversary roll call

4 Pioneer riders

5 The first touring team

6 The forgotten test match

7 Jack Barnett – part-time champion

8 Wal Phillips – what an experience

9 Tommy Price – World Champion

10 Speedway in Wales

11 The Scottish Scene

12 Argentina and Frank Varey

13 Speedway in South Africa

14 The Promoter – the buck stops here

15 Track preparation

16 Referees viewpoint

17 Reminiscences of a Senior A-C.U. referee

18 The Machine Examiner

19 The Track Announcer

20 Speedway tapes: a new entertainment

Team records

Team champions

Strange facts

Notable firsts

The Veteran Dirt Track Riders Association

Foreword

Ron Hoare knows all the gallant pin up boys who caused such flutters in feminine hearts of the thirties. He has gathered together stories from past champions, near champions and stars of maximum illumination who brightened the speedway scene many moons ago. I wish Ron's book the greatest success. Although this is not, of course, his first literary venture, anyone who sits down to a task of this kind needs pluck, luck and a winning ticket in the Pools for his effort.

There has been a sudden emergence upon the book writing scene previously occupied solely by such as World Champions Ivan Mauger, Barry Briggs and Peter Collins plus of course, Dave Lanning, Cyril May and the best selling author who writes these notes (!) and this bears out my recent prophetic utterance. THE NEXT FIVE YEARS will see such staggering support, such a return to the days when every Stadium was packed to the rafters on speedway nights, that the veterans will be shocked into unbelief. Every new book written, every television and radio broadcast, every movie about the sport is an indication that speedway is in for boom times undreamt of even in the days when Frank Varey, Claude Rye etc. were heroes to their massive following. Jack Parker the plausible, will, of course, say his piece and reckon he knew all along that the next half century of speedway would see riders in the millionaire bracket and that he was born forty years too soon. Poor Jack, we could almost cry!

I welcome Ron Hoare's book – may it prosper progressively.

Johnnie Hoskins

Johnnie Hoskins

Introduction

It is, I suppose, the ambition of most speedway writers and historians to produce a comprehensive history of the sport and perhaps one day I may tackle this monumental task. However, this book is not intended, indeed it was never intended, to be even a potted history. It is, perhaps, more than anything else an expression of gratitude to the men who made possible the great sport that we know today – those incredible characters who in days of packed stadiums, had the thousands of fans yelling for more. I felt, quite simply, that speedway's most unique occasion, its Golden Jubilee, which we have just celebrated, should not be allowed to pass without paying some sort of tribute to these pioneers who from so very many walks of life, ventured into the unknown. A number of them were just content to see the game through its teething troubles and then slip quietly from the limelight, others stayed long enough to see it take its place amongst the country's major sports and there were some who went on to become great champions.

However, the book is not merely concerned with the past, although I think it only right and proper that the old cycling track at Epping Forest should be prominently featured, as it has become to all real speedway enthusiasts what a strip of the Hampshire downs has become to followers of that other great summer sport, cricket. Much space, obviously, is devoted to those riders who have become legendary heroes, many of whom I am proud to number amongst my friends, but in addition you will find contributions from and interviews with some of the sport's present day personalities, each of whom tells you something of his own particular job and experiences in the world of speedway. I am most grateful to all of them and I hope there will be items of interest for everybody – the statistically inclined, the historically minded or those who just like reading about their favourite sport.

Ron Hoare

Acknowledgements

The majority of the photographs reproduced in this book have been provided by Wright Wood, to whom the author is indebted. Other photographs have been loaned by Cecil Bailey and Alf Weedon from their private collections. Where known, the name of the original photographer has been acknowledged. To these gentlemen too, the author wishes to express his appreciation.

No W C **11**

Date......*July 6th*..............1928

Received from Mr. E Pink

the Sum of

TWO SHILLINGS & SIXPENCE

Membership Fee for WHITE CITY SPEEDWAY CLUB, *Season* 1928.

For International Speedways, Ltd.

....

SPEEDWAY CLUB SECRETARY.

This Receipt constitutes your Membership Card and Temporary Pass, and should be produced as your authority to enter the Speedway for practice and racing purposes.

A White City (London) 1928 pass – two shillings and sixpence. Messrs. Dugard and Dunton please note!

1
Down memory lane with Johnnie Hoskins

Do you remember 'Dusty' Haigh, a most delightful fellow with a flow of language unsurpassed? His method of conveying information was so studded with odd adjectives, it was quite impossible to understand what he was talking about. I rather prided myself on my own lurid language, but compared with the easy flow and rhythm at Dusty's command, I had to admit being second rate.

One well remembered night at Hackney Wick, there was the usual excitement at a match against the local rivals, West Ham. Dusty Haigh and Bill Clibbett were partners for the Hackney side, Tommy Croombs and Ken Brett for the Hammers. Enthusiasm was tremendous as the teams struggled for supremacy; it was one of those matches which really electrified the vast crowd.

And then it happened. All four riders crashed together and all four were lying among the still spitting and spluttering machines. A cloak of silence suddenly descended on the scene as the crowd waited breathlessly. One by one the riders rose, but one would ride no more. Dusty Haigh, dear old Dusty, was lying there with blood streaming from nose and ears and as I took his hand, I knew he had gone to that other land. We carried on with the meeting and said never a word to the crowd, but all the steam had gone from the match. Riders knew and the spectators, in that uncanny way they have of sensing the truth, filed sadly from the stadium to wait for the next day's papers.

A couple of years afterwards, I was with a clairvoyant and she said 'There is a man here with a message for you.' Then after a pause she stood with her hands to her ears as if unbelieving and gaped. 'I can't understand a word he is saying. He speaks in a broad northern dialect and his language is peculiar.' I smiled to myself and said 'That would be my old friend, Dusty Haigh.' I never got the message but I was happy in the knowledge that Dusty was enjoying himself and still speaking in his own delightful way among the heavenly hosts.

We are so immersed in our own everyday affairs that we seldom reflect upon that which comes to all of us, when our earthly walkabout arrives at the end of the road. At the annual gathering of Veteran Riders when the Chairman announces his regrets that another of the old timers has passed over and we stand for a moment in silence, there passes through my mind as in a flash, the memory of hundreds of riders I have known. As the wine flows and merry chatter goes on around, I see the smiling faces, the mischief in the eyes of unseen guests as, in imagination, I visualise each one and recall a joke here, an argument there or a piece of horseplay before an appreciative public.

Some riders, because of their personalities, their deep impressions on the fabric of the mind, rather than their ability to win races, stand clear cut in our memories and whole books could be written about some of the heroes of the speedway over its half century of progress. We still have heroes in the making, youngsters emerging from nowhere in particular yet destined to be listed amongst the names of the world beaters of their time.

So life goes merrily along from day to day and year to year. As the great performers and many of the top teams of the twenties and thirties they mean nothing to the youthful enthusiasts of today. In another half century the Ivan Maugers, the Peter Collins, the Ole Olsens and such will mean nothing to the supporters of the year 2028.

A few, a dwindling number of veterans, remember with nostalgia the great ones like Dusty Haigh ....

Johnnie Hoskins in a light-hearted
mood 'assisted' by Bill Longley

Dusty Haigh

2

Birthplace of British dirt track racing

THE CLUB WILL HOLD A DIRT TRACK RACE MEETING ON FEBRUARY 19th AT THE 'KING'S OAK' SPEEDWAY WHICH IS EASILY ACCESSIBLE FROM LOUGHTON OR CHINGFORD. THERE ARE EIGHT EVENTS AND A GOOD ENTRY HAS BEEN OBTAINED. THE FIRST RACE STARTS AT 10.30 am.

No one at that time could have envisaged that this brief announcement in the **Motor Cycle** magazine dated 16th February 1928 would herald the birth of what is now one of the country's major sports. Much has been said and written about this historic meeting but let Freddie Law, later to ride for the High Beech track and eye-witness on that memorable occasion, take you through the day.

"One of my favourite pastimes in the late twenties was riding around on my Norton and one morning in February 1928 I elected to go through Woodford on the way to Epping Town. To my astonishment, the Epping road was packed with motorbikes of all sizes and shapes, all travelling in the same direction – never before had I seen so many machines on the road so early in the year. Being inquisitive, I stopped and discovered that a new type of sport was being tried out at High Beech and so I decided to attend the first dirt track meeting held in this country and organised by the Ilford MC and LCC.

I doubt very much whether anyone attending that first meeting will ever forget it. By the size of the crowd, it seemed that the whole surrounding district had turned out to witness the new entertainment. It was held under conditions that would not be tolerated today either by rider or spectator. The centre of the track was a football pitch and on this particular morning it was a sea of mud – to say that we were to see real dirt-track racing was stretching the imagination a bit, as the centre of the track was absolutely crammed with people who were also packed tightly round the outside of the circuit. I am sure that the organisers of the event, even in their wildest dreams, hardly expected to see such a crowd, and I think it says much for their enthusiasm that the racing ever got going under such conditions. However, the meeting did eventually get under way but we were to see very little of it – onlookers were crammed so tightly that after the riders passed, they spilled all over the circuit and had to push themselves back off the track each time the riders re-appeared! It is amazing that any of the competitors finished the course and that there were no serious accidents to spectators. However, the full programme was somehow completed and so that morning saw the birth of dirt-track racing (later to be known as speedway racing) under anything but ideal conditions and as we now know, the sport had come to stay. One outstanding personality of this and many other meetings was the late Jack Hill-Bailey and the sport owes much to men like him who gave so much of their time and labour in those very early days.

Anyway, I had seen enough to feel that I would like a go at this new sport, but the only machine I had at the time was a 16H Norton which was unsuitable for racing, so my first job was to find a suitable bike. In the end I placed an order for a 350 cc Cotton with a Blackburne engine. The Cotton arrived and after having joined the Ilford MC and LCC, I was given a trial at High Beech and duly signed up by the Club. In those days it was quite an ordeal preparing the machines for racing – being standard road vehicles we rode them to the track and then removed all unnecessary equipment such as mudguards, lamps, brakes and the nearside footrest. After racing finished, the bikes were re-assembled and ridden home sometimes in a rather battered state! By this time almost every make of motorcycle was being used on the track, the majority being ordinary road machines. In those teething days. Colin Watson rode a New Imperial and he could certainly drive it around at a great pace but the favourite during 1928 was, of

13

SOUTH MANCHESTER MOTOR CLUB

AFFILIATED TO THE A.C.U. THROUGH THE NORTH WESTERN CENTRE,

ANNOUNCE A

DIRT TRACK RACE MEETING

ON A LARGER SCALE THAN HAS EVER BEEN PRODUCED

A Restricted Race Meeting held under the General Competition Rules of the A.C.U., by virtue of Permit No. R105 issued by the A.C U., North Western Centre, and Supplementary Regulations contained herein.

A Member of any Club affiliated to the
North-Western Centre (A.C.U.) can compete in this event.

TO BE HELD AT

AUDENSHAW RACECOURSE,

Ashton Old Road, Audenshaw, Manchester,

On Saturday, March 3rd, 1928, at 2 p.m.

The whole interest of the Motor Cycling world is focused on this class of event.

Steward of the Meeting: A. HOGGART (S.M.M.C.).
Timekeeper: A.C.U. TIMEKEEPER.

Here is a glorious opportunity for you to become acquainted with this class of Racing, shortly to be specialized in by our Colonial Visitors.

☞ OVER £50 IN PRIZES. ☜

AWARDS.

3 SOLID GOLD WATCHES (15 Jewelled Movement), value £7/10/- each.
6 CANTEENS OF CUTLERY, value £3/10/- each.
6 SOLID SILVER CIGARETTE CASES, value £1/10/- each.

In departing from the usual practice of presenting Cups and Medals for more useful and valuable awards, we are quite prepared to award Cups of same value if the winners so desire.

PRACTISING WILL BE ALLOWED ON SATURDAY, MARCH 3rd, from 12 to 1 p.m.

The front cover of an entry form giving details of an Audenshaw Dirt Track race meeting held on March 3rd 1928

course, the Douglas. Amongst its adherents were Ed Farley, Syd Edmonds, and Jack Barnett whilst Les Green and Norman Humphrey favoured the Ariel, Jack MacDonald had a BSA, Digger Pugh a Dunelt and Phil Bishop and Roger Frogley both relied on Rudges.

As the season progressed, more tracks were being opened and High Beech riders took part in the initial meetings at London venues such as White City, Wimbledon, Stamford Bridge and others and during Bank Holidays we sometimes rode in three meetings during the one day. I remember one Saturday at High Beech when two men arrived from Birmingham, mounted on BSA's, Jack Parker and Bert Perrigo, and if my memory serves me correctly, Jack had just won the Colmore Cup. By the end of the first season, the riders felt it time to form an association for their protection, this body was known as the Dirt Track Riders Association and I still have a book of rules. During the following year, when league racing came into being, I invested in a James 500 cc twin speedway model but was soon to regret it – this particular model had a habit of shearing the crankpin. I used to wire James at Birmingham, who would despatch a crankcase assembly by passenger train and I often sat till early hours of the morning to get the bike ready for the next meeting! At the end of '29 Glanfield Lawrence arranged for a party of us to try out a new Rudge speedway bike at Brandon and it went so well that I decided to get one in time for the 1930 season. It certainly proved the best machine up to that date and I was doing very well until someone came down in front of me at West Ham and landed me in Poplar Hospital with a severely damaged knee. Injuries were far more numerous in those days of course, but it was a great life whilst it lasted!"

So there we are – straight from the horse's mouth, if Fred will excuse the expression!

Whilst on the subject of that never-to-be-forgotten meeting, I can remember that legendary character, the late Billy Galloway, the 'Demon Barber', who actually competed, telling me a year or two ago, and with typical humour, about his experiences. "I did a great deal of racing in my time starting in West Maitland, NSW on an Indian Scout and graduating to England, Scotland, Egypt and France but my most memorable and frightening experience was at the High Beech opening in February 1928 when thousands more spectators turned up than was expected. They stormed on to the grass inside the track which was marked off only with white paint and possessed no safety fence whilst people climbed trees on the outside, some falling on to the track.

When the competitors tried to ride the white inside line, onlookers couldn't move back so they literally had to draw in their stomachs! To make matters worse for me, I had no bike of my own so I was loaned Freddie Dixon's IOM Douglas, complete as he had ridden in the TT races with the same gearing. Being a hairdresser by trade, I knew nothing about gearing – with my Indian all I had was a twist grip and a button (magneto cut out) – so here I was sitting on the IOM Duggie whilst the London agent tried to tell me that this lever was for air, that lever was for the magneto, that thing on the tank was an oil pump and those on the side were the gears. So off we went first time out and the pushers off were shoving me and the bike began to backfire and flames shot out of the carburettor with everyone yelling push, push faster. At last we got going but I couldn't get out of bottom gear! With these sort of problems plus the crowd inside the track, it was certainly a day to remember!"

Ivor Creek, one of the top Englishmen during the late twenties and thirties, also rode that day and had his own special memories not only of that first encounter with a speedway track, but of subsequent events.

"This little story begins around 1927 at C.F. Temple's offices in London's Marble Arch when Stan Glanfield and a friend took possession of Temple motor cycle combinations and began a round the world endurance trip. A visit to Australia was of course a must and it was there that they came across a thriving new sport called dirt track racing which they found fascinating and as a result the Aussie promoters were invited over to Temple's showrooms where hill-climb star Jimmy Baxter was Sales Manager. Baxter, who was a leading light in the Metropolis MC Club, of which I was a member, then got together with the Ilford club and this is how the first meeting became possible and a most unique one it turned out to be. It was not the sort of speedway track you would know today, merely a type of cinder and grass arrangement with spectators all around and some lodged up in the trees. That day I appeared on a camshaft Norton and there is a fairly well-known picture of myself leading Fred Ralph mounted on a Coventry Eagle, although he eventually got past me on the last turn of the five lap race. The winners received only a trophy and for my victory in the fourth event, I was given a pint tankard with the embossed emblem of the Ilford MC and LCC stating that it was the first meeting held in this country. The second demonstration of the new sport took place in April at Greenford, on a trotting track which was more of a bona-fide cinder track and one third of a mile instead of a quarter. One of the participants was Billy Galloway on a Douglas, who emerged as the fastest man on the day. Billy, of course, came over with the original Aussies and worked his ticket on the ship coming across as a hairdresser.

However, I was duly signed up by the newly formed Company for the princely sum of £3 per week and £1 for every race in which I started, together with any prize money that I might win. The first track which the Company opened was at Celtic Park, Glasgow on 1st May 1928 at which a number of local boys took part and speedway had become established in Scotland. On 15th of that month, I won a Golden

A photograph of the historic High Beech meeting held on February 19th 1928 (Motor Cycle)

A panoramic view of a 1928 meeting in progress at High Beech

A view of Zamalek Speedway, Cairo, in 1928 which Ivor Creek and Billy Galloway helped to build

16

Sidecars on the huge Greenford track 1928

Gauntlet and £20 which was quite a sum in those days and we really had a party that night! Just after that we were joined by more Americans and Aussies like Sprouts Elder, Paddy Dean, Buzz Hibberd, Spencer Stratton and so on. Meanwhile, the sport was really catching on in England – Wolverhampton and Crystal Palace came in and the most famous lady rider of them all, Fay Taylour, made her debut at West Ham. Altogether that year, I was present at the opening of about fourteen tracks – Newcastle, Rochdale, Edinburgh, Warrington, Birmingham, Exeter and many others. It was all great fun and the last opener at which I appeared was Banister Court, Southampton in October.

Naturally, as winter was on its way, we began to think about where we might go during the close season and in conjunction with Wolf Barnato at Hyde Park – he was a Director of the Egyptian Greyhound Racing Association – we decided to gather a team of about 18 riders and Billy Galloway and I were elected to go on ahead to try to get a track constructed in Egypt. So off we went in the early part of November to contact the would-be promoters in Zamalek, Cairo, where we were landed with the job of showing them how a speedway track should be laid and shaped inside the existing dog track. This was great fun as with the usual speed at which the Arab works, with the use of a rake and a basket, it looked as if it would be several years before a racing strip would be ready! With a little bit of ingenuity, we managed to introduce some more up to date tools and by obtaining some cinders from the local generating station, we began to get things moving but the next problem was to get all this hammered down so that it made some sort of hard surface. A motor car with the cricket pitch roller on the back was tried, but it only bounced its way around and next they produced a steam roller, but not a small one – a twelve tonner! And believe me, as this place was on low ground, it wasn't long before it had sunk in up to its firebox and come to a grinding halt! Well, something had to be done and although I had never driven a steam roller before, now was my chance to learn! So with the support of the rice-man who put a long tow rope on the front of the roller we mustered all the available native labour and after a head of steam had been raised, I got in the control box, opened the throttle and with a few puffs and a lot of shouting by the rice-man, we moved out of the hole. After this hole had been filled, we managed with a slightly smaller roller to complete the job ready for the team when they arrived later that month.

There was one big difference in the racing in Egypt compared with ours. As everyone knows, the Arabs are keen betting types and they quickly set up a totalisator at the track with some rather peculiar results but racing never really caught on and it all folded up about two months later. Some of the boys went back to await the start of the English racing season but Bill and I liked the sunshine so much that we stayed on, Bill getting himself a job with the Jowett people out there and I with the Austin Morris works. There we remained until it was time to return for the new season.

After we got back to England, we found more and more speedways coming into being, including Wembley (I remember very well the ope. ing of the Empire Stadium) and heard that another company had been formed known as 'World Wide Speedways' – all in all it was quite a boom year. At the end of 1929, we sat down once more to work out our winter plans and hit on the idea of a South American visit. A team was raised under the management of A.J. Hunting, including Max Grosskreutz, Frank Varey, Frank Duckett, Bob Harrison, Oliver Langton, Buzz Hibberd, Arthur Jervis etc., and our destination was the Speedway Huracan in Buenos Aires. This tour did in fact last for the whole of the 1929/30 winter and was pretty successful but Latin American crowds can be very excitable, to say the least, and the fences were wire

17

Ivor Creek (C.F. Wallace)

Billy Galloway

covered all the way right down to the pits to prevent bottle throwing and possible invasion".

During that winter, Ivor and his merry band formed themselves into four teams and raced mainly against each other, although a few of the local hopefuls such as Juan Pagano and Roberto Sigrand were occasionally drafted in.

The evolution of the speedway engine has always been of great interest to Ivor. 'Of course, to start off with, we used our own road machines stripped down but they were just ordinary bikes with a gearbox which was not really satisfactory as we had to change gear whilst going along. Soon bikes were introduced with gears which you could change by varying the sprocket sizes and thus remain in that gear throughout the race. As a result, you could then select the correct gear ratio by changing the sprocket to suit the conditions and size of track.

One of the early bikes was, of course, the Douglas, which was a corruption of the RA Sprint model and the OC TT model made by putting the OC engine into the cycle parts of the RA model, by altering the engine plates. This became more or less the standard Douglas speedway machine. They were pretty spectacular as they had a fairly long wheelbase and therefore slid a good deal more than the shorter wheelbase jobs and produced the thrills. The first single that came out was built by Rudge and was known as a Dirt Track Special – this was quite a good machine but it had a short wheelbase and a tendency to flip one over the handlebars at the slightest provocation. It became known to the riders as a collar-bone breaker, but after altering the frame, bending the down tubes and shunting in a little bit more on the cross tube to alter the steering head angle and the trail, a machine was evolved which handled much better, slid well and had good performance. It was afterwards improved upon still further by Martin's, who put in a JAP engine, and it soon became **the** speedway machine, to remain in vogue for many years. One of the early foreign machines that came in was, of course, the Peashooter Harley, which was of only 350 cc with two short exhaust pipes belching flames and ridden I think, by Cecil Brown and Buzz Hibberd. Then there was the Indian single cylinder favoured by Art Pechar, but this one never really got off the ground, possibly because of the low capacity of the engine. Scott's also had a go and these bikes made a nice noise but apart from Frank Varey, riders did not find them all that satisfactory and they soon faded from the scene. So the machines today are very much the same as those developed from the original Rudge.'

A third rider to take part in that historic meeting was Alf Medcalf who turned out to be the fastest man on the day. Alf seemed to specialise in 'firsts' as he was at the Harringay, Wimbledon and White City (London) openings – a very busy man was Alf in those experimental days, but he took it all in his stride as he was practically brought up on a bike. His father was an agent in Colchester and Alf joined the local motor cycle club as soon as he reached the prescribed age. He put in a lot of practice on the Lowestoft sea front on his 'Duggie', gained further experience with hill-climbing and at one time had one of the old belt drive Nortons.

Asked about his favourite track, Alf spoke of his **least** favourite – his unlucky track, White City (London). Alf reckons that every time he rode there something happened to him and it all culminated in a badly broken leg when he clashed with Max Grosskreutz one evening – a mishap which forced him to give up the game. One amusing story he tells of the West London track occurred when he had trouble about twenty yards from the finishing line and actually pushed home a bike in flames for third place!

His best days were at Harringay, where he rode with the Spencer brothers, Eric and Stan. The £5 appearance money plus points money which he used to receive made life reasonably comfortable. Alf's most prized possession is probably a cup which reads 'Awarded for the fastest lap – First British Dirt Track Races – High Beech, 19th February 1928.'

High Beech in 1929
Colin Watson (left) is mounted on Frank Arthur's Harley Peashooter alongside Jack Barnett before their match race. Jack won by 2 runs to 1. In the centre is Jack Hill-Bailey, responsible for the early High Beech meetings (Sport and General Press Agency)

20

3

Golden Anniversary roll call

As speedway's Golden Anniversary has been so much in the news, a great deal will have been heard or written of those who blazed the trail and whose names will live as long as speedway survives. Come with me on a walkabout, or if you prefer it, a nostalgic stroll, and meet some of these men who have played such a significant role in putting the sport on the road to its present popularity.

Let us start in the Midlands which has always been a hotbed of motorcycling, where speedway in particular has produced so many fine riders. We will begin with BILL ASHCROFT, if only for the reason of alphabetical superiority! A real pioneer is Bill – a member of the first Birmingham league side at Perry Barr. In common with many of the early riders, he suffered broken collar bones, ribs etc., often due to the rough and bumpy tracks, but one rather different spill which he always remembers and relates with typical humour, happened not on the track but in the pits area. "I pushed my Duggie to start the engine, gave it a little more throttle than intended and the machine shot forward. I made a flying leap, missed the saddle and landed astride the rear tyre with the wheel revolving but my leather trousers saved me from a fate worse than death and I got away relatively unscathed. It really shook me, I can tell you!" Another amusing story that Bill tells was when he was tuning his engine in a friend's garage on the main Stratford/Birmingham road. He decided to give the bike a run out, wheeled it onto the main road, gave a quick look round to see whether the coast was clear and roared off for a two or three miles sprint before returning to the garage. Bill continues the tale. "Unfortunately, a policeman that I hadn't noticed in a shop doorway had witnessed the whole event and on my return booked me for riding a motor cycle without a silencer, without brakes, tax, insurance, number plates and for driving dangerously! When the summons arrived, I did not attend but wrote to the Magistrate and explained that I was pushing the motorcycle to put it into a van, but the engine fired (being a dirt track racing machine). Consequently, the only way I could control it was to leap quickly into the saddle, otherwise not being fitted with a clutch or brakes, it could have become out of control causing danger to others. Due to the absence of brakes, it took some distance before the bike could be stopped. The remarkable sequel to this was that they accepted every word – I could hardly believe it! What the poor old copper thought of it I will never know – I shudder to think what would happen if someone did the same thing today." The ex-Perry Barr rider remembers the early practice sessions at Hall Green which he attended with an ex-TT Douglas (clutch and brakes removed) and was told by the pit man "You'll never get in a race with **that** thing", so he ordered a DT Douglas from the Colmore Depot. To run in the engine he used to push it about a mile to a local club cricket ground and belt it round the outer perimeter. The authorities never knew of course, otherwise, as Bill says, they would have strung him up!

He has poignant memories too of the Billingham Dirt Track Depot at Kew Bridge, which always gave a first class service and provided accommodation whilst they stripped engines and fitted new pistons ready for the next London meeting. It was whilst coming home from London with his old captain, Wally Lloyd, in Wally's Austro Daimler at about midnight that the trailer came adrift and they watched it career across the road and disappear over the hedge with two Duggies aboard! Those were the days!

DENNIS BRANDISH, one of a family of top motor cyclists, performed on his 500 cc AJS at the old Lythalls Lane track on a surface composed of reddish ash. Dennis tells of one particular meeting on the local track. "During a race, I lost my petrol filler cap on the bumpy track and the vibration from the engine shot alcohol over vital parts of me – when the race was finished, spectators must have been puzzled at my antics!" Dennis has the amazing record (especially for an ex-speedway rider!) of possessing a clean driving licence from the day he took up driving – not a single insurance claim or even a parking offence!!

Jack Parker has held the Match Race Championship longer than anyone else. Here he is once again receiving the Golden Helmet with unsuccessful challenger Aub Lawson on the left (G.W. Jones)

Over to the famous Midlands motorcycling brothers, HARRY and CYRIL TAFT. Harry, former Birmingham skipper, did the Midlands rounds – he also starred for Leicester under Syd Jackson before moving with Syd later to Coventry. His match race battles with the giants of the early years such as Gus Kuhn, Frank Arthur and Arthur Jervis were worth travelling miles to see.

Harry recalls the opening night at Perry Barr. "There was a terrific spirit amongst the English riders, although we still had so much to learn. For this night, I had to collect my bike – a Sharratt – from West Bromwich where they were made and this particular machine had been used during the afternoon for motorcycle football leaving the engine still warm! I took the 70 mph Sharratt down to the track, removed the silencer and other bits and pieces and got ready for the evening. I managed to win the 350 cc Final and then met the great Sprouts Elder in a match race, receiving eight seconds start, but I came off on the second lap. Sprouts was a tremendous performer. His handling of his machine was about the best in the world just then and this skill allied to his apparent disregard for life and limb made him the No. 1 attraction everywhere. Elder's style was guaranteed to make hearts miss a beat, but he had an amazing knack of getting out of trouble. If we had four thrill makers of the calibre of Elder in the game today, there would be no difficulty in maintaining gates."

Brother Cyril, another pioneer, spent most of his league career with the Brandon outfit, but his numerous trips abroad proved very lucrative and he was at one time Champion of Spain.

Then there is FRED WILKINSON former Leicester Super specialist. There were few who could match Fred on the old one-third of a mile circuit at Melton Road – what a pity the track had such a short life as there has never been a racing strip quite like it. After his retirement, former grass track and hill climb star Fred settled down to managing his own business and to a life of public service, during which he became a local councillor. Incidentally, apart from his prowess on road and track, Fred also found fame at motor cycle football and of all things, musketry!

To talk of the Midlands and not mention PHIL (Tiger) HART would be unthinkable. Emigrating to Australia at the age of 16, Phil was back the next year in company with Steve Langton to try his luck at the speedway game. They were introduced by the late Clem Cort to Johnnie Hoskins who took them under his wing – Phil has nothing but praise for the way Johnnie treated these two nervous youngsters who had been earning 30/- a week in the Bush. He got them bookings at Portsmouth and helped Phil to find a niche at Kings Oak where he rode as partner to the King of Crash, Phil Bishop. After the war, Phil captained Birmingham and still retains a great affection for that Club – he was in fact, team manager a year or two ago He reckons one of the highlights of his long career and one of the most enjoyable of his tours, was the

22

The last of the great leg trailers – Oliver Hart (J.S. Grace)

ENSA trip which he made to Germany in 1945–46 with a bunch of top-notchers including Norman Parker, Ron Johnson and Eric Chitty.

One of Phil's pet stories is of the time when he was riding for West Ham. After the meeting was over, he was first in the dressing room, changing surprisingly quickly and when the other riders came in for their baths, he emerged fully dressed. I need hardly tell you that the Custom House boys' reaction to this was to grab Phil and hurl him into the bath, clothes and all! Phil crawled out and disappeared into the changing room dripping wet. Little did they know that Phil, anticipating this little joke, had donned other people's clothing, one article from each dressing room peg, before entering the the bathroom and so when the riders later came to put on their clothes, one had a soaking shirt, another sopping wet socks, another saturated trousers and so on. When they tried to find Phil to vent their fury, needless to say, he had vanished into thin air!

Like a great many of his contemporaries, Phil has done a lot of things in his time, including stock cars, speedway promoting and car sales ventures and he has at present a flourishing insurance company. One of the first ideas Johnnie Hoskins had when Phil came to him for help was to christen him 'Tiger' in typical Hoskins fashion and to this day he is still 'Tiger' to many of his friends.

BILL STANLEY is another of the Midlands pioneers. "I had heard of the new sport that the Australians introduced to London and decided that an early visit was a must so with a friend I found myself outside the White City Stadium at Shepherds Bush. Our luck was in for within minutes we had met up with Jack Parker and Bert Perrigo who were riding there, helped push their machines into the pits and were 'in' at our first meeting. We liked it so much that we stayed overnight, went to Harringay, then back to Birmingham and the Alexander Sports Ground at Perry Barr where the Sunbac club had laid out a cinder track. After a couple of evening practice sessions, I entered the first official meeting on my 500 Ariel road bike, won the Handicap race and was presented with my prize – a black and white five pound note – and that's how it all started!

Soon afterwards, I won the Shirley Club Cup at Hall Green but perhaps my biggest moment was when I made the Brandon side, teaming up with such great and likable fellows as Lew Lancaster, Wilmot Evans, the Parker brothers and of course the one and only Tommy Farndon. The incident I most remember during my stay at Brandon was of the day when most of the team lost their machines – the lorry taking our bikes to Lea Bridge for a league match went up in flames between Stony and Fenny Stratford and all but two of our motors were destroyed. All traffic was held up pending the arrival of the Wolverton Fire Brigade and the road was blocked for a mile on either side for more than an hour. The 'Brandon Monk',

Norman Evans, equally well known in London as he was in his native north-east

Jack Parker's colleague at the BSA factory – Bert Perrigo. He was the factory trials ace

Gordon Byers

Harry Whitfield

24

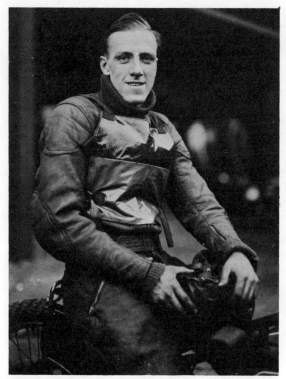

George Greenwood

Sid Hipperson

Bob Ibbotson leads two Swindon riders at Long Eaton in 1950

the team's mascot which was being carried in a cage, was rescued unharmed and not in the least perturbed! Frantic telephone calls to Stan Glandfield of Brandon Speedway, who was a partner in the big motor cycle firm of Glanfield Lawrence, produced seven machines including one belonging to Frank Arthur and considering all things, the team did pretty well, losing by only 30 points to 22 at the East London track.

One enjoyable feature of the London trips was the get together on the return journey at the Watling Street transport cafe, where many a race has been re-run over a plate of bacon and eggs! After leaving Coventry, I had a spell in the Metropolis, gaining a medal with Stamford Bridge under the captaincy of that great gentleman Frank Arthur, and enjoying a particularly happy period at Plymouth with a fine bunch of lads including Australians Bert Spencer and Frank Pearce, Ted Bravery, Bill Clibbett, and Jack Jackson.

I used to look forward to week-end trips to Rotterdam organised by Jimmy Baxter, where the English boys were always welcomed, but soon after this, I returned to Birmingham where the spark began to fade and I decided it was time to quit. I have never regretted those years of racing and have certainly never forgotten the great sense of comradeship that existed between most of us."

Another legendary figure in the area is SQUIB BURTON. One of England's most brilliant riders in the early thirties, Squib still reckons his greatest achievement was to ride at nine meetings in a single week! This included two meetings on a Bank Holiday Monday and another couple on the following Saturday – certainly a case of stamina allied to skill.

Squib started off his career at Lythall's Lane and then began his association with Leicester, to become one of the stadium's most famous personalities – he had a very successful time both as a promoter and a rider at Blackbird Road. He had a spell with Sheffield after Leicester's first closure and then a short run in London before hanging up his leathers. Nowadays, the sprightly Squib, looking half his age, runs his garage business and is the local Chairman of the Bench.

Before we leave the Midlands, there is one name that we could not forget and so almost last but never at any time least, we come to JACK PARKER. What can one say about Jack Parker that has not already been said a dozen times before? Match Race Champion for donkey's years, National Speedway Champion, Speedway Riders Champion and so on and so on, a man who was longer in the top flight than any other rider in the history of the sport. It is interesting to hear his views on various tracks (and he must be more knowledgeable on this subject than most). He rates Belle Vue as England's best track, but his greatest love was the Sportsground in Sydney which he reckons was the finest the game has ever seen. Jack feels very strongly that a novice rider should learn his trade on a large track – he considers that most young riders who have been taught solely on a smaller than average course become small track experts and little else. He illustrates his point by listing all the really good riders who started off on the big circuits, and has the greatest admiration for the fast, round-the-fence stars like Syd Jackson, George Newton and Oliver Hart. In fact, Jack feels that as they had to cover a lot more ground, they should have been entitled to more money than men like himself who rode the line (I fancy that Jack's tongue was in his cheek when he told me this!)

Speaking of J.P. leads us almost automatically to BERT PERRIGO. One of the oustanding all-rounders of his time, Bert's spell in speedway was confined mostly to Birmingham, but his exploits in the world of motorcycling are legion. He was already a trials rider of some repute before joining the BSA firm and he and Jack Parker went on to record numerous successes in the team events including the International Six Days Trial. It was Bert who set off with Jack to High Beech in a motorbike and sidecar to see what the new sport was all about – a journey which resulted in Jack making his first appearance on the dirt.

Heading South we meet up with TED PINK another of the real 1928 pioneers. Ted had a fair amount of success on the grass before dabbling in the new sport and turned out at that first Greenford meeting in April 1928 on a half mile trotting track, the surface of which consisted of large lumps of ash and clinker! They had a few amusing characters at that huge Middlesex venue, one of them a gentleman using the pseudonym of AJ Stripes who turned out to be the son of a South American diplomat.

One of Ted's most vivid recollections was the first appearance at Greenford of the famous American Art Pechar. With the local boys all watching attentively, he appeared in beautiful black shiny leathers (the homespun riders were at that time clad in whatever they could get hold of!) and proceeded to do a few touring laps before returning to the pits for adjustments. Then out again and did another gentle lap or two before coming back again for more adjustments. Once more he appeared, did a couple of laps and decided that the time had come to demonstrate his prowess for he suddenly opened out and began to perform the most fantastic broadsides which had the locals, spectators and riders alike, goggling – a series of beautiful slides breaking the ,track record, putting it up to 52 mph upon which he improved as the season went on.

Ted, incidentally, had the only existing Velocette at Greenford, but a great variety of machines were tried out at this large circuit including AJS, Harley, Douglas, BSA, Rudge, Raleigh, Matchless, a 350 cc

OK, James, a 500 HRD Calthorpe, 350 Chater-Lea and a Cotton ridden by Les Blakebrough whom Ted rates as the best of the local men.

Next, ARTHUR (Westy) WESTWOOD, that great showman and man of many parts. Arthur is very clear about his first ride – he was working with the Anglo-Persian Oil Company when he decided to return to England and called in on a speedway meeting at Wolverhampton. He liked what he saw and thought he would have a crack himself so he borrowed a bike from Jack Wolfenden who was then promoter at Monmore Green. Arthur jumped on and approached the bend, tried to turn but nothing happened and he went straight over the fence! However he began to show some potential in practice, so much so that he was offered £10 to ride in a meeting proper, given half a lap start in his first ride but by the end of the evening was up with the best men and was dazed when he found that he had won the incredible sum of £30 by the time the meeting was over. Sharratt's then built him a special speedway bike in exchange for 25% of his earnings, which Arthur thought fair. He gained a place in Hall Green side although he got a telling off from his father, who wanted him in the family business. However, Arthur was beginning to smell success on the 'dirt' and decided to concentrate on riding. He got bookings on many tracks and when he was signed up for a match race with that fantastic showman, Sprouts Elder, he began to feel that he had really arrived! Sprouts, incidentally, never earned less than £100 a meeting in those days and more often it was nearer £200.

It was in 1931 that Westy started his trips to France where he became kingpin at the Buffalo Stadium and later promoter-rider. He had one more spell in England when he joined the Clapton outfit at Lea Bridge which, under the captaincy of Jack Parker, was one of the most attractive teams in the league. He later quit riding to concentrate on promoting. It was whilst he was running the old Leeds track that he organised special trains from Leeds to his other track at Sheffield for 2/- all in (1/- fare and 1/- entrance fee) but this facility was discontinued after a while as Arthur found that he was bringing 2,000 people by train, but only about 500 were going to the speedway, the rest having a cheap trip and staying in the town! Sheffield at that time had its own dance hall and many of the famous bands of the day played there, including Henry Hall. The Leeds track was next door to the football club at Elland Road and was the first to have its own milk bar and other streamlined refreshment facilities.

At the outbreak of war, Arthur was responsible for the entertainment of troops in France and after the evacuation from Dunkirk in 1940, he continued in the same capacity for Southern Command and produced 'Private Smith Entertains', one of the most popular of radio programmes. When speedway recommenced, he operated a track at Tamworth, which was constructed out of a cricket field and furnished with a great deal of equipment from a local US Army depot.

LEN PARKER will probably go down in speedway history as the last of the original Douglas exponents, for he stuck to the Duggie when all around him were resorting to the more modern JAP. As this machine had brought him success from the very early days at Bristol and Cardiff and during his league stint at Wimbledon naturally he never really felt the same about the JAP. Speedway formed the continuation of a fabulously successful career in all forms of motorcycling – TT races, hill climbing, road racing, sand racing, speed trials, grass track racing – you name it, Len did it! After the war, Len took to four-wheeled competition, but a serious smash finally put paid to all that.

Ex-Sheffield stalwart TOMMY BATEMAN is remembered mainly for his fine performances in the North of England, although he was in fact a member of the Hackney Wick side that won the Division II Championship in 1938. It is not generally known, however, that Tommy first took to the cinders as far back as 1929 and thereby hangs a tale. Having heard that a speedway track had been constructed at Rotherham, Tommy, who was working at a garage, bought a 1911 Scott from his employers for the sum of £2! He rigged it up as a speedway machine by removing all the extras and practised broadsiding on loose straw in the stack-yard of his father's farm – his dad raised no objection to Tommy having a go on the track as he probably considered that on a bike of that age the lad could not possibly come to any harm! For his first ride, Tom and a friend towed the Scott about 40 miles to the track and he finished third in his initial outing, then went on to beat a fellow competitor in a match race. His opponent was mounted on a Douglas and they passed each other seven times before Tommy got the verdict by two lengths. Following this Tommy had a fall and another third place and by the end of the evening he found that he had won thirty-five bob. Considering his weekly wage at the garage was only 25/-, he felt on top of the world.

After a few months during which he won the Skid Skinner Silver Helmet and the Hunt Cup, the Yorkshire-born rider took to the grass and it wasn't until the mid-thirties that he made a come-back to the speedway game, later becoming Sheffield's most consistent scorer until a frightening accident finished his career – a spill in which he nearly lost his life. Although the later years found him a much more accomplished speedman, Tommy claims the pioneering days were always the most exciting when, during his early outings at Rotherham, the programme included such colourful names as Cyclone Smith, Hurricane Harvey, Crasher Edwards, Tearaway Bill Styring and Wrecker Reed.

Memories of the old Southampton Saints are conjured up by the name of VIC COLLINS. Vic started his motorcycle career on a BSA road bike, joined the Southampton and District Motorcycle Club and in October 1928, was riding at the new Wymering Park racecourse where he won the Scratch Race for bikes up to 600 cc. In the same month, Banister Court opened its doors to dirt track racing and in the following year Vic became a member of the original Southampton side, with Jimmy Hayes, Tommy Cullis, Clarrie Eldridge, Cecil Bounds and many other well-known southern based riders. Despite breaking a leg during the early part of 1930, Vic came back tremendously to win the Golden Gauntlet Championship at his home track's final meeting of the season from a class field including Tiger Stevenson, Roger Frogley, Phil Bishop, Arthur Warwick, Ron Johnson and Reg Bounds. Vic was another of the early riders who bridged the gap between pre-and post-war speedway and he made a come-back in 1947 to turn out for his old side when they re-entered the league.

Grass track ace ROY DUKE rode at many of the non-league tracks before the war – Wisbech and Bell End amongst others – and was known as the 'Duke of Bell End' due to his outstanding performances at the Holbeach circuit. After finishing third in the Eastern Counties Grass Track Championship, he decided to break into league speedway and after the war gave sterling service to Norwich, Yarmouth and Leicester – the latter side was then known as the 'Hunters'. Roy gained the team's first win after they re-opened for speedway in 1949. He has affectionate memories of the old Dagenham track where he rode with Frank Hodgson (father of Belle Vue rider, Russ) but despite winning so many trophies and prizes on the grass, he reckons his greatest achievement was losing to Bill Kitchen in a best of three series of match races. Bill was of course, one of the three top Englishmen just before the war, and Roy put up a tremendous show before losing narrowly in the third and deciding race.

Moving eastwards, we meet up with ARTHUR WARWICK, the former sidecar expert who took to speedway and made a great success of it. His interest in the chairs came at a very early age as his father had an old 1914 4¼ hp BSA two-seater sidecar – actually Arthur managed to start the machine at the age of 8! He later joined the Manor Park and District Club, took up grass track and road racing and rode solos and sidecars in the Isle of Man TT races. After going to see the new dirt track craze, he immediately became involved by purchasing a Douglas, but quickly changed to a Rex-Acme with a Rudge engine and then moved to a Rudge frame with a JAP engine. During the early Stamford Bridge days, Arthur enjoyed a great deal of success with his sidecar outings, but when the first Stamford Bridge speedway team was formed, he became a member and helped them to their championship win. He gained a number of international caps but retired fairly early to concentrate on his business although he retained his interest for many years in the Amateur Dirt Track Riders Club, of which he was a Vice-President.

Arthur lists his favourite tracks as Stamford Bridge and Wembley, but it was at Lea Bridge that he recalls a most unusual race with Roger Frogley – Roger on a solo and Arthur with a sidecar! On a specially laid deep track, they passed and re-passed but Roger just made it by a length.

No one who saw that brilliant West Ham side just before the war will ever forget ARTHUR ATKINSON. 'Akko' as he was popularly known, first rode a motorbike at the age of 12, showing his brother's licence whenever he was pulled up! He got his first run out at the Blackpool trotting track and made the Leeds league team at seventeen years of age. It was the great promise that he showed which prompted Johnnie Hoskins to bring him down to Wembley and then to take him across London to West Ham when Johnnie moved on.

With Bluey Wilkinson as his partner, Arthur improved enormously and these two won the Coronation Gold Cup – a top event for team pairs – in 1937. By the time 1939 arrived, Arthur was one of England's top men and a great season made him favourite for the World title in September but a month or so before the Final was due to be run, Arthur sustained a broken collar bone at Wimbledon. In order to qualify for the last stage, Arthur still had one meeting to go and with typical Yorkshire grit, turned out with the shoulder strapped. Despite the discomfort and pain, he scored maximum points to make quite sure of qualifying. As we all know, this effort was to be in vain due to the intervention of war.

It seems a far cry from Wembley to the old Barnsley track where Arthur can recall riding on a cinder track surrounded by a turf safety fence in his extreme youth! West Ham figures mostly in his reminiscences, which is understandable, when one considers that it was at the Custom House that Arthur met his wife Tippy, who was working as a secretary. Mention of West Ham also brings to mind the well-known story of the time when American ace Jack Milne met with an accident whilst racing there and had his thumb ripped off. It was reported that later that evening a track raker found the thumb and gave it to Johnnie Hoskins who immediately dropped it and fled from the track! I have always regarded this little tale as apocryphal, but Arthur confirms every word of it. After all, he was there!

One story that Arthur tells seems quite incredible, but fortunately, he took it all in good humour. When visiting Sweden in 1938 he was invited to participate in a championship meeting at Gislaaved and had little difficulty in winning all his races. At the prize presentation dinner afterwards, he was told that because the local favourite had made fastest time of the meeting, he (Arthur) would receive only second prize and the local Swede would be presented with the winner's trophy! Can you imagine that happening

Wally Hull shows them how at White City, Manchester in 1929 (Thomson Publications)

in England?

Moving North we come to one of the greatest thrill-makers in post-war speedway, OLIVER HART. The last of the great leg trailers, he spent most of his riding life with Belle Vue and Bradford, apart from one brief spell with Wimbledon immediately after the war. One of the most cheery and friendliest men in the game, he won a lot of admirers and was voted the most popular rider during the late forties.

Often called 'Laughing Boy', Oliver was forced to retire whilst still at the height of his career, due to a serious accident at Sheffield in the mid-fifties, when he broke his back. But he has had the odd ride since 'just for fun', notably when Hackney held a celebration meeting in 1968, and in the second half Oliver raced away from the opposition.

WALLY HULL was another avid motor cycle fan from his most tender years. His dad owned an old two-speed Levis and whenever he was away, young Walter would jump on it and roar round the garden, to the horror of the neighbours and the utter dismay of the gardener. So to preserve everyone's sanity (and of course his machine) Mr. Hull Senior bought his son and heir a model of his own as soon as possible. Wally got in some road racing, some sand racing at Southport and a bit of other competition work before taking to the cinders at Audenshaw. His first meeting brought him a brand new five pound note and Walter decided that he was on to a good thing. His second meeting found him the recipient of fifteen pounds and he was now certain that he was made for life!

One of the great jokes at Belle Vue was Wally's camel bike. Whilst he was starring at the other Manchester track, White City, he got himself a Rudge Special but it was not very much use to him because of his unusually long legs. As Walter himself put it "My knees seemed to want to dig trenches" so when he moved over to Hyde Road, he had a go at designing a frame himself, which became known as Wally's camel. Although it became the object of a great deal of fun, the fact remained that it was the only machine that Wally could ride effectively!

Despite his successes at White City and Belle Vue, where he was chosen to represent his country, Walter still rates Wembley as his favourite track where he held more than one record in the early thirties.

ROL and MAURICE STOBART the North-West 'twins' have spent most of their life in the area. Elder brother Rol, in a career that spanned 20 years, recalls riding in 1930 at Holker Street, Barrow, on a track composed of cinders laid on grass with a safety fence about two feet high and made up of corrugated sheets with sharp points at the top – he has a photograph to prove it!

Rol has many tales of the old Preston track. German Bill Kellner who spoke very little English, figured in an incident which produced a few laughs for the boys. He was travelling through a very busy London street and suddenly jumped out of his car to obey the call of nature, leaving it exactly where it was in the middle of the road. A policeman came up and there was he and Bill, with his very limited English, remonstrating. However, after a while, the copper gave up trying to understand Bill's comic English and hand signs and the German got away with it! Another story of Preston that comes to Rol's mind is of the home stars, Ginger Lees, and Joe Abbott, who were returning home from a London meeting driving Chrysler cars with trailers. As quite often happened, they became involved in a friendly race home but after Joe had taken the lead, Ginger suddenly drew level and made frantic signs and gesticulations. However, Joe who suspected the usual trickery, ignored him and drove on even faster. At the end of the journey, Abbott pulled up and found that he had lost his trailer some 50 miles back!

A lot of Rol's personal memories are of his spell with West Ham. "Alex Dovenor, then Manager, gave the riders an end of season dinner at the posh Frascati's Restaurant in the West End. Arthur Atkinson had already sold his car prior to a trip to Australia and was cruising around for the last few weeks in an old banger – a Morris saloon from his farm with plywood in one side window, a side lamp tied with string etc. Arthur drove Alex and I to the dinner and when we arrived at Frascati's, the Commissionaire looked the other way – later on it must have been quite a sight to see us all getting out of that wreck sporting evening dress and Alex in his tails!" Another of Rol's highlights was helping to make the speedway film **Money for Speed** starring Ida Lupino and John Loder, with fellow riders Cliff Parkinson and Gordon Byers. In one scene Rol was asked to drive straight at the fence when coming out of the first corner – actually he was only required to travel a few feet and then pull up, but when he saw the film later on, it was quite horrific to see the bike go on and the dummy depicted as himself hurtle over the fence.

Perhaps the best known of Rol's adventures was the 'Ride to York'. When Johnnie Hoskins heard that Arthur Atkinson was to buy two ex-police horses at the sales, a publicity stunt was inevitable and Jim Stenner of the **Daily Mirror** was very quick to step in. The horses were paraded at their home track (West Ham) on speedway night and next morning, Arthur and Rol rode the horses round the track, over the dog racing hurdles and off along the same route taken by the notorious Dick Turpin. Rol was astounded at the reactions. "We stopped for breakfast at Hampstead Heath and continued on our way now closely followed by the RSPCA. Letters of protest came from as far afield as New Zealand objecting to the cruelty inflicted on the animals in making them attempt such a lengthy journey, but nobody said anything about the cruelty inflicted on us, for after the first day our bottoms and legs were so sore that we wondered if we would be able to stand upright again. Although Johnnie Hoskins had issued some blah about me being a member of the North-West Hunt or something, I had no idea how to ride a horse! We were advised to apply cream to our backsides during the ride, but I think we should have used grease! It was quite a palaver at the stopping points applying cream to the offending areas, but on the second day, one of the horses went lame and both were put on the train home. You have no idea how thankful Arthur and I were to be able to wend our way wearily back to our families!"

Rol goes on. "I remember a certain trip to Buffalo Stadium in Paris when a few of us were invited over. We travelled from Victoria Station via Newhaven to Dieppe and when we arrived we found that the organisation was nil. It was simply a question of You, you and you ride for the Championship of Europe! Anyway, we had our fares paid and £36 for the trip, which was acceptable prize money then."

Workington Speedway ran in the early days at Lonsdale Park and continued rather spasmodically until the late thirties – the last couple of seasons it was administered by the dog racing company in conjunction with Rol himself and featured riders of the calibre of George Greenwood, George Pepper, Charlie Spinks, Norman Hargreaves and so on. Rol was probably the most successful of them all over this period but the venture itself was not really a financial success. "My efforts at promoting were not exactly prosperous for apart from Workington, I put on a meeting at Ayr and another at Carlisle and in both cases it was the one and only! My riding career terminated at Edinburgh when I fractured my skull and after five weeks in Edinburgh Royal Infirmary, I thought it time to call it a day."

Brother Maurice, who shared in some of these adventures, has a little more to add. "Some of my own recollections include the time when I was riding for Newcastle. Although things got a bit rough occasionally, sportsmanship was always very high and I can remember towards the end of one league match, I accidentally squeezed my partner Reg Hay into the fence. Reggie was justifiably annoyed and in the scratch race that followed after the interval, Reg's blood was up. During our heat I sat behind, watching him cut Syd Littlewood to pieces. He was so engrossed in his task that I managed to slip through and win the race. When we came back into the pits, Reggie came across and said 'I thought it was you I was doing up' and then added 'Come on it's not worth falling out' and shook hands. That's how it was in those days. I remember too, colliding with an Australian rider and getting the black flag, but when the Aussie picked himself up from the track, his pants were torn off revealing a bare backside!

Another adventure occurred when Rol and I were on the way back home from Newcastle in my car, a round axle Chrysler that was notorious for bad steering. A bit of drizzle made things a trifle slippery and

30

when we came to a corner at about 60 mph, we couldn't take it. The car went out of control and we hit the wall, doing about three somersaults. Amazingly, we got out little the worse for wear and the first man on the scene was from our home town of Aspatria. He helped to get the car back onto its wheels and we loaded all the stuff back, gave it a push and much to our surprise it started so that we continued homeward at 60 miles an hour! Believe it or not, but that is true!"

Naturally, Maurice recalls vividly his first rides on the dirt – at Barrow on a Douglas. Having ridden on the sand, he could slide the bike a bit and he won his first race against three other novices and was put into the heat of the Scratch Race against Bill Kellner, Len Myerscough and another rider. He led for three laps before letting them through, which earned him a booking at York. As this was in the early thirties and depression was still with us, he didn't own a set of leathers, his gear consisting of a pair of whipcord pants, about half a dozen jerseys which he used one on top of the other for protection and a pair of boots! "The result" says Maurice, "was that I looked a bit of a rag bag. However, I did so well that night that the pushers who had ignored me to begin with, suddenly started to fight for the right to push me off! The star man then was Chun Moore, who later rode for Belle Vue and Sheffield.

My most frightening moment? I think this must have been at Harringay before the war, when the meeting was cancelled after six heats. The management refused to refund any money and the crowd were threatening to wreck the joint and everyone in it, which included us. Fortunately, the ringleaders were calmed down after promises from the management and we all got out safely. What a night!"

Another from Lakeland is CHARLIE BARRETT, who started his career at Middlesbrough and came South to join the Wembley Lions. He went to Exeter with the Wembley team to play the locals in 1930 and his first look at the big circuit with its sweeping bends took his breath away, but when racing got under way the Lions proved a wee bit too strong for the home side. Riding with Charlie that day were Norman Evans, Cliff Parkinson, Stan Catlett, Art Warren and his partner Bert Fairweather. Top men for Exeter in those days were Buster Buckland, Noel Johnson and Charlie Swift. Charlie made periodic visits to the Madrid track; at that time with King Alfonso on the throne, Spain was a Mecca for British riders and the game was put over in a big way, with tracks like Madrid and Barcelona well up to standard. The Spaniards really got worked up and regarded speedway as more dangerous than bull fighting.

Over to another Northerner, JACK GORDON, who before turning to Speedway, rode successfully at the Nantwich Grass Track – the best known Northern short circuit of that time. He joined Belle Vue before the war, but is best known as one of Middlesbrough's mainstays during the early post-war years and later as Captain of the Wigan outfit whose track was forced to close after an all too brief spell in the Second Division of the old National League. In that all-conquering 'Boro side of 1946/47 were such fine riders as Frank Hodgson, Kid Curtis, Wilf Plant and Geoff Godwin, in addition to Jack himself.

The North-East is represented by that formidable foursome Gordon Byers, Jack Ormston, Harry Whitfield and Norman Evans – a quartet of famous ex-Wembley Lions.

GORDON BYERS was presented with his first bike on his fourteenth birthday, a second-hand Douglas, which marked the beginning of his career as a motorcyclist. He moved on to reliability trials and then learned the art of broadsiding at Edinburgh, under the tuition of Drew McQueen. Gordon started speedway seriously at Newcastle – in fact, he took part in the first Brough Park meeting as a 16 year-old and became a sensation almost overnight, winning the North-East Coast Championship after only a few months in the saddle. Son of well known trials rider, A.W. Byers, Gordon later moved to London where he really made his name with Wembley. He went on to form with Ginger Lees one of the game's famous partnerships and to ride for his country in test matches.

JACK ORMSTON is one of those men who seem to have done everything. His speedway exploits are renowned. After commencing at Middlesbrough, he succeeded to the captaincy of Wembley and became the first London Riders' Champion. Jack went to Australia with the first English team to tour down under and in fact skippered them in two tests and won a World Champions series in Sydney that same season. After this, he went off to Canada and America and then returned home to England where he gained many more international caps before retiring to go back to farming.

His love of horses comes out strongly, which is no surprise as he has owned racehorses since 1930 and has achieved as much fame as a trainer as he did as a speedway rider. In addition, he has taken part in countless point-to-points, hunter steeplechases and fox hunts.

Then there were Jack's flying days and he talks of the time when he and Roger Frogley bought an aeroplane which Roger, on his very first trip, managed to crash on his Hoddesdon farm with co-owner Jack looking on! Jack was, in fact, a first class pilot, taking part in the King's Cup and gaining second place in the Grosvenor Cup Air Races.

Ask NORMAN EVANS who is the best all-round rider he has ever seen or ridden with and he will plump unhesitatingly for Bill Kitchen, former Wembley skipper and pre-war Belle Vue star, partly on account of Bill's uncanny ability to cover his partner for countless five-ones. Norman, a Middlesbrough man, spent a considerable part of a very useful career in London and after the war skippered Newcastle,

Harry Taft (C.F. Wallace)

Cyril Taft (C.F. Wallace)

Wilf Plant

Ted Pink on his Velocette

Frank Lawrence

Jeff Lloyd (on bike) with brother Wally (C.F. Wallace)

Jack 'Bronco' Dixon

Roy Craighead

but apart from being a very handy rider to have around, Norman was a great humorist which leads neatly on to a little story. As many people know, the lot of a team manager, like that of W.S. Gilbert's policeman, is not always a happy one and can at times be a little embarrassing. I remember the late R.M. (Sammy) Samuel, one of speedway's most brilliant journalists, recounting a tale involving a bunch of riders which I believe included Norman. Sammy was often called upon to look after a party from London bound for the North of England and in this instance it was necessary for the team to stay overnight after the meeting. As the local hotels were fully booked, accommodation was found for them in a guest house. During the night, one or two of the extroverts amongst the party got up to a few pranks and it all became a bit noisy, so in the morning the lady who ran the show gave them all a piece of her mind. Furthermore, she showed her dislike for them by the measly breakfast which she provided and the size of the bill with which she presented them. On the journey home, Sammy had the distinct feeling that the riders concerned had got their own back in some way, but everyone was very tight-lipped and it was not until he was called before a Board Meeting of International Speedways, that he found out exactly what had happened. Every rider had devoted his own portion of marmalade to the lubrication of the works of her priceless grandfather clock and any over had been well spread around the inside of her piano! (Norman says he was not guilty!).

HARRY WHITFIELD still lives at Middlesbrough where he commenced his riding career although he very soon moved down to Wembley. Harry was one of that small band of men who were rated as 'stars' in 1929 and barred from the original league sides because they were considered too good! He eventually did receive permission to turn out for the Lions. It was whilst with Wembley that he paired up with George Greenwood – these two were the first to perfect the art of team riding – and played a leading part in the Lions' hat-trick of championship wins (1930–31–32). Partner GEORGE GREENWOOD was one of the great stylists of his time. Although he was a very young member of the first Leeds side it was at Wembley that he really made his name. One of George's finest performances was when he topped the England score chart in the second test match of 1932 against a rampaging Australian team who were virtually unstoppable. In fact only he and Jack Ormston were capable of holding the Aussies on the night. It was during this match that a famous 'incident' occurred. An entirely unsatisfactory start to Heat 12 caused George and his partner Tom Farndon to slow down and stop in anticipation of a re-run but to everyone's amazement, the referee allowed the race to continue thus presenting the Australian pair, Dick Case and Billy Lamont with a 5-1 win. When the results went up on the scoreboard, the huge crowd voiced its disapproval for several minutes, the announcer gave up and eventually the board was lowered and the next heat started without any announcement being made.

Another of the fine batch of early Northern riders was ERIC BLAIN. Eric, who began his riding career at Warrington, usually managed to link with teams containing outstanding performers. He made his league debut with Liverpool where he teamed up with men like the brilliant Ginger Lees and Les Wotton. At Sheffield he rode in the company of Squib Burton and Dusty Haigh and at Belle Vue of course, Frank Varey, Eric Langton, Max Grosskreutz. Probably Eric's best season was in 1933 when he finished the year as Sheffield's top pointsman.

Speaking to Eric of his early experiences, two episodes came quickly to mind, neither of them particularly pleasant! The first was a very expensive occasion when his engine blew to pieces whilst he was competing in a heat of the Jubilee Cup at Belle Vue. "Bits of metal were flying around like shrapnel" said Eric. "A piece of the cylinder wall struck a pillar in the stands right in front of the heads of a number of spectators. Undoubtedly, the pillar saved them from very serious injury." The other incident occurred when a spate of pilfering in the Sheffield pits culminated in the disappearance of his bike. Later on, purely by chance, Eric noticed some spare parts in the boot of a car and on closer examination found that they were from his own machine and were being smuggled across to France to be used as spares at the two or three French tracks in operation at the time.

Associated with Eric in those palmy Northern days was FRED DAVENPORT, a Warrington warrior under the captaincy of George Milton, who became a familiar figure around the Lancashire tracks. There was also ARTHUR JOHNSON, who performed with distinction at the early Birmingham meets. Arthur was included in the Perry Barr team for their first ever league match.

Heading back south, we meet up with the remarkable CLAUDE RYE. Claude's introduction to speedway was via White City (London) where, after trials, he gained a two-year contract at Preston. But he is best known as one of the most popular pre-war Wimbledon riders. His track career was cut short not only by a succession of injuries but due to the fact that his flourishing business was taking up more and more of his time. However, during those riding years, he skippered the Dons for a spell, represented his country and rode in Germany, Denmark and France where he won a meeting billed as an unofficial 'World Championship', an event which he remembers with some affection if not a little amusement!

Claude rode with and against all the great names of the mid-thirties and is not alone in choosing Vic Huxley as the greatest rider he has ever seen. He had plenty of opportunity to watch and study his team-mate, the great Australian maestro.

34

Today, Claude is known throughout the world as the managing director of Britain's largest ball bearing firm, dealing with Russia, Japan, USA, Germany, Italy, Argentine – you name the country and Claude has contacts there! His brothers Horace, who had a few outings with Wimbledon, and Percy, who turned out with his younger brother at Preston, have been associated with his 'empire' which all began with a tiny motorcycle shop and went on to make him a Freeman of the City of London. But it is Claude Rye, the spectacular leg-trailer, who is still remembered by many at Plough Lane.

ALEC SLOW is the only survivor, or at least the only traceable member, of the 1930 Lea Bridge league side which contained such popular favourites as Jimmy Stevens, Howie Osment, Alf Foulds and Australian Harold Hastings. Alex turned up at Lea Bridge during the summer of 1928 when young men who fancied themselves as riders were invited along one Saturday for trials at the track constructed around the football ground where Orient (at that time Clapton Orient) paraded their skills during the winter months.

"Quite a crowd of fellows turned up wheeling a motley collection of bikes" grinned Alec. "Mine was a 500cc BSA 'sloper' and when practice commenced, I spent most of my time off the machine and was very surprised when I was offered a ride the following week. I turned out for the Lea Bridge league side the following year during their first league campaign and also the next year when I bought a JAP-engined Rudge. This was not a good move as I had endless trouble with shedding and breaking chains. Later the manufacturers produced a chain with triangular outer links (rather like a chain saw) which improved matters a great deal. However, I came off one evening and my left hand was caught between the chain and sprocket and sustained quite a bit of damage. As I had been a fairly successful saxophonist before I took to the cinders, and as one needed ten fingers to play the instrument, I decided regretfully that I would return to the music business and give up my track work.

Lea Bridge was a particularly friendly place with great rapport between riders and spectators and it is a bit unfortunate that it is remembered by some people as the track where betting was introduced. During that infamous season, the A-CU were very tough and riders who participated there had their competition licences withdrawn and could not ride at any other track. Consequently, none of the top class riders took part but there were enough volunteers to enable meetings to be run. However, the venture failed after a few months and the track became 'legitimate' again.

I remember on one occasion riding at Wimbledon where, during the evening, a large bump developed in the track which the grader could not cure. This resulted in many spills and I found myself cutting a groove in the cinders with my nose, having taken to the air over the handlebars. In the next day's **Evening News** the Speedway column was headed 'Malcolm Campbell sees speedway rider break nose' and I have always wondered what difference that made! Next morning, they dug up the track and found a surveyor's tripod buried beneath the cinders!"

Whenever American speedway riders are mentioned, the first names that come to mind are more often than not those of the Milne brothers but a rider who is sometimes overlooked is RAY TAUSER from Oregon – ex boxer, wrestler and parachutist. Globe trotting Ray was an extremely fine performer on the track and rode in something like eight countries, which was not bad going in those days.

Ray has a collection of interesting stories – for instance when he found himself unwittingly driving a car for a bootlegger during the prohibition days! "I got out of that pretty quickly" said Ray, "and later, when Speedway had obtained a hold in the States, Johnnie Hoskins and a few of us tried to put the Sport over in Madison Square Garden. It was Johnnie, incidentally (who else?) who abbreviated my name from the original Tauscher to Tauser so that it would roll more easily off the tongue."

Then there is the almost unbelievable story of the time when Ray and Jack Parker tried to obtain a couple of beds for the night but found the hotels full. They finally found one which seemed to be short of a receptionist, so Jack and Ray wandered around and got themselves a room, bedded down for the night, and in the morning arose and walked out without seeing a soul!

Ray began his speedway career in this country with Wembley, but will be remembered (a) for his very successful spell with Wimbledon and (b) for the time when, against all the odds, he staggered the speedway world by becoming 'Star' Riders' Champion at Wembley. To achieve this, he disposed of most of the favourites in the early heats and then pipped Huxley in the Final. Unfortunately, just as he was reaching his peak over here, the Board of Trade withdrew his riding permit and Ray, who was most unhappy with their decision, never returned to these shores as a rider.

Although sometimes overshadowed by the sheer brilliance and personality of elder brother Jack, NORMAN PARKER was without doubt one of the finest riders of his time. Arguably Wimbledon's greatest skipper, Norman was responsible for the swift development of so many young riders, an outstanding example being Ronnie Moore who was brought over from New Zealand by Norman and taught the finer points of the game. Although he is still in touch with speedway, Norman's main interests these days are in the scrambling exploits of his younger son and the running of his public house in Northampton.

These are just a few of the legendary giants without whom speedway would have folded up long ago,

Maury Mattingley after winning the Scottish open
championship. Behind him are the runners-up Eric Boocock
and George Hunter
(A. Dickson McLaren)

Bill Gilbert

Frank Hodgson

Phil 'Tiger' Hart speaking at a Veteran Riders dinner

Two top-notch 'Hammers' – Tiger Stevenson and Arthur Atkinson

leaving memories of a mere circus stunt. They came through some pretty tough times and before we leave them, perhaps we could mention a few of the others who have never lost their interest in the sport that they graced.

SID HIPPERSON, for instance. Ex-Norwich and Leicester favourite, Sid reckons that he has broken more bones on the track than the man reputed to hold the record, the late Phil Bishop. Often seen at Leicester meetings is WILF PLANT, once of Middlesbrough, Fleetwood, Wimbledon etc. Wilf, a very dependable rider in his time, gets around the tracks with his son Graham, recently with Halifax.

HARRISON GILL rode at Droylsden and the Audenshaw Racecourse right at the beginning and will argue with anybody that speedway (or dirt track) really began in the North! Another of the sport's characters, Harrison is still very much part of the Belle Vue scene.

BERT FAIRWEATHER distinguished himself by winning the very first race when the Empire Stadium opened for speedway in 1929 and rode for the Wembley team in their first year, although he had signed on as a mechanic. He finished fifth in their averages that season which, incidentally, went on until 28th November! Who says that our modern season is too long? Another pioneer, JACK PARSONS, rode up at Newcastle soon after the Brough Park track opened its door, but emigrated to Australia. He carried on riding down under for a while and stayed in touch with the Australian scene.

BOB LOVELL, post-war Birmingham star, gave great service to a number of clubs, including Harringay, Bradford and Bristol. A spectacular leg trailer, Bob's best spell was probably with the Perry Barr side which included men of the calibre of Tiger Hart and Stan Dell. Ex-Wembley and England International GEORGE WILKS made up a formidable spearhead with Tommy Price and Bill Kitchen during some of the Lions' greatest years. George still retains a very active interest in vintage motorcycles.

RON HOWES started off as a Wimbledon mechanic and later 'did' for Vic Huxley before taking to the cinders himself. One of his most treasured possessions is the set of leathers that belonged to the great 'Hux.' After the war, Ron turned out for West Ham, but when Rayleigh Weir Stadium opened its doors for racing, he was appointed their first skipper and became a great favourite with the Essex crowd.

BOB IBBOTSON was another to be associated with the opening of a track – in this case Long Eaton. Unfortunately, he was involved in a horrific crash at Cardiff in 1951 and sustained multiple fractures of the skull in addition to broken ribs, collar bone, hip and pelvis. Considering the extent of his injuries, Bob made a remarkable recovery although he was never able to ride again.

Next JEFF and WALLY LLOYD, amongst the most famous of speedway brothers. Elder brother Wally still holds a unique record – he was not yet eighteen years of age when appointed leader of the Birmingham team and is the youngest captain the game has known. Often styled 'The Mighty Atom', he represented his country and had a tremendous spell just after the war with Belle Vue when he, Jack Parker and Eric Langton made up a most respected trio of heat leaders. Jeff in a fine post-war career with Newcastle, New Cross and Harringay, was one of England's leading lights during the late forties. He can remember when very young, going along to see his brother perform and wielding an oil rag, which was all he was allowed to do! It was seeing all the great ones in the pits that made young Jeff determined to have a go as soon as he became of age.

There have been many other characters over the years, who have left their mark on the sport – VIC LONSDALE, the 'wild man' of Bradford, Workington etc., who had the crowd roaring whether he was winning or tangling with the fence and GEORGE SAUNDERS, ex-West Ham, Hackney, Wimbledon and Wembley middle order man was another value-for-money merchant. Cheery George is still as much of a character today as he was in his riding days. How about that delightful personality, 'The Champ' himself, HOWDY BYFORD, whose whole-hearted efforts as well as his singing (!) made him so popular with London crowds. RON CLARKE, the Londoner who won so many Yorkshire hearts during his great spell as Bradford's skipper after the war – the combination of 'Clarkie' and Oliver Hart couldn't fail to raise a laugh. JACK COOLEY, speedway rider and stunt man who lost count of the number of times he tore down the fence, fearless FRANK LAWRENCE, game battler for New Cross whose refusal to accept defeat made him a man to be reckoned with and GEORGE WIGFIELD, the tough Northerner who proved such a doughty fighter for the pre-war Sheffield outfit. JACK 'BRONCO' DIXON was another Sheffield favourite who also served Belle Vue so well – one more example of the classic breed of Northern racers. Smooth riding FRANK HODGSON, former king of the Dagenham track who made such an impact at Middlesbrough (Teesside), VIC PITCHER and JOHN CARPENTER who did so much for Leicester after their re-opening in 1949. Super clubman DANNY LEE, so well liked in Edinburgh where he helped to re-form the post-war Monarchs, ROY CRAIGHEAD and BILL GILBERT both members of the all-conquering Wembley Lions who lost only one League title between 1946 and 1953, and mechanical maestro MAURY MATTINGLEY enormously popular not only down Southampton way, but also up at Coventry, Wolverhampton and Glasgow, where he skippered the Scottish side during their first British League season at the old White City track. Maury used to fly from his Hampshire home to Glasgow every week to lead the Tigers and was the first Englishman to win the Scottish Open Championship, a feat which he accomplished in 1963 with a

Jack Gordon (Southern Photographic Service)

Danny Lee

Bill Stanley

The start of the 'Dick Turpin' ride.
Arthur Atkinson jumps a fence at
West Ham Stadium whilst Rol Stobart
looks on (Planet News)

Rol Stobart winning the cup at Barrow in 1930. Note the safety fence with the sharp points at the top (British Photo Press)

15 point maximum.

I doubt whether many old West Hams fans will have forgotten TOMMY CROOMBS, the quiet man of Speedway, who thrilled the East London fans in those palmy pre-war days. Tommy earned the name of the 'White Line Wizard' due to his ability to hold the inside of the track at top speed. He spends a lot of time these days with son Bobby (ex-New Cross and Wimbledon) at their business in Dorset, that most pleasant of counties, which is the home of several distinguished speedway names such as ex-British Individual Champion, 'TIGER' STEVENSON, another great Englishman of the early days and BRIAN CRUTCHER, one of the two youngest men to qualify for a World Final and who so nearly took the coveted title in the middle fifties.

There are other notable names like all-round motor cyclist ALF HAGON, one of the fastest men seen on two wheels, still operating his famous World Track Racing Service, LES 'SMILER' WOTTON, who gave first class service to so many clubs, the tall ARCH WINDMILL that great fighter for the cause of Hackney and later Wimbledon, Manchester-based WILF LUCY who later became mechanic to Peter Craven and CECIL BAILEY, ex-scrambler, who made such a sensational debut at Southampton in the early post-war years, jumping from novice to heat leader inside six months after being spotted by Frank Goulden, Saints star of yesteryear. Cecil's travels included trips to Amsterdam and Milan and one incident on the Dutch tour still brings a smile to his face when he recalls that great joker Phil Bishop arranging with their car driver to pull up right by the side of the canal when it was very dark, so that a certain rider opened the back door and stepped straight into the drink! His excursion to Italy for a three-night stand started well enough as they were conveyed from their hotel to the Milan track in taxis on the opening night, but the meeting was not too well supported and on the second evening they were carted off in a small three wheeler bus, to perform before an even smaller crowd. As a result, the third evening found them waiting in vain for transport and they eventually made their own way to the track by tram!!

Cecil has a lot of memories of the Banister Court track, but he talks of one particular time that really brought him down to earth. During a spell in 1949, the Saints were carrying all before them and took on a team of ex-Southampton riders in a special challenge. In his first race, he was up against Jack Parker and Alex Statham, but he made the gate and was in the lead coming out of the first corner. Using all his knowledge of the track and knowing where the grip was, he entered the next bend feeling supremely confident when whoosh! Jack went one side of him and Alex the other and that was the last he saw of them. Cecil never forgot the lesson he learned that night.

Here then are just a few of the headline makers who still retain their interest in the game that they helped to build or consolidate. They and others like them saw the Sport through its good days and its bad days and it is difficult to imagine how speedway could have survived without such men of personality and character.

H.R. (Ginger) Lees, a great and consistent performer for Preston and later Wembley

4

Pioneer riders

Over the next two pages I have set out to do the impossible! It was just 50 years ago when team racing began, since when league speedway has been the sport's mainstay over the years. In view of this, I have attempted to compile a list for posterity, of the men who made up these 1929 sides, most of which competed in the first leagues formed in that year. Included in the list are the 'Star' men, both English and Australian, who were banned at the commencement of league racing but eventually received permission to take part.

Although I have spent a great deal of time trying to avoid mistakes, there may perhaps be names conspicuous by their absence. To those who been overlooked, I hope my sins of omission will not be taken to heart – my apologies to them. Here then is my tribute to those who really started the ball rolling.

SOUTH
Jack Adams
Bill Albert
Frank Arthur
Stiffy Aston
Ronnie Baker
Jack Barnett
Jack Barrett
Tony Barrett
C.S. Barrow
Dick Bellamy
Len Bellamy
Lou Berger
Dicky Bird
George Bishop
Jack Bishop
Phil Bishop
Les Blakeborough
Bert Bolt
Frank Bond
Cecil Bounds
Reg Bounds
Maurice Bradshaw
Bill Bragg
Charlie Briggs
Cecil Brown
Hilary Buchanan
Buster Buckland
Louis Bull
Nick Carter
Dick Case

Stan Catlett
Sid Chambers
Alf Chick
Larry Coffey
Vic Collins
Fred Cooper
Clem Cort
Dudley Cox
Crasher Coxhead
Ivor Creek
Harold Crook
Tommy Croombs
Bill Crouch
Tommy Cullis
Charlie Datson
A.W. Day
Vic Deale
Les Dearth
Will Dennis
John Dinsmore
Clem Dixon
Frank Dobson
Bryan Donkin
Roy Dook
James Douglas
Frank Duckett
Don Durant
Syd Edmonds
Sprouts Elder

Clarrie Eldridge
Cyril Emms
Don Everness
Dank Ewen
Doug Fairbairn
Stew Fairbairn
Bert Fairweather
Ed Farley
Colin Ford
Del Forster
Alf Foulds
Joe Francis
Buster Frogley
Roger Frogley
Dudley Froy
Syd Fuller
Bert Gerrish
Stanley Gill
Eddie Green
Max Grosskreutz
Hurricane Hampson
Morian Hansen
Wally Harris
Harold Hastings
Jimmy Hayes
Wally Hicklin
Buzz Hibberd
Bern Hieatt
Ron Hieatt
Ivor Hill

Jimmy Hindle
Freddie Hore
Fred Howsley
H.F. Hudspeth
Norman Humphrey
Vic Huxley
Charlie Jackson
Jack Jackson
Noel Johnson
Ron Johnson
Irvine Jones
Jim Kempster
Nobby Key
Jack Kidwell
Allen Kilfoyle
Charlie King
Gus Kuhn
Billy Lamont
Fred Law
Harry Lewis
Eric Lister
George Lovell
George Lovick
Jack Luke
Bruce McCullum
Les Maguire
Roger May
Ernie Mayne
Alf Medcalf
Dick Melville
A. Merrell
Reg O'Connor
Nick Nichol
Jack Ormston
Fred Osborne
Tom Osborne
Howie Osment
Len Parker
Ray Parsons
Frank Pearce
Ernie Perry
Wal Phillips
Ted Pink
Jimmy Pink
Reg Pointer
Pip Price
Steve Pullen
Fred Ralph
Ray Ralph
Len Reeve
Ernie Rickman
Crawley Rous
Alf Sawford
Dennis Seaman
Mart Seiffert
Triss Sharp
Ivor Sinclair
Eddie Slade-Jones
Jimmy Sloman
Alec Slow

Brisbane Smith
Dicky Smythe
Bert Spencer
Eric Spencer
Stan Spencer
Charlie Spinks
H. Standish
Reg Stanley
Jimmy Stevens
Tiger Stevenson
Col Stewart
Charlie Sticpewich
Alf Summersby
Charlie Swift
O.E. Sykes
Ray Tauser
Don Taylor
Geoff Taylor
Stan Taylor
Charlie Traynor
Howard Traynor
Wally Trumble
Ben Unwin
Champ Upham
Albert Wakerley
Art Warren
Arthur Warwick
Colin Watson
Bill White
Harry Whitfield
Bluey Wilkinson
Taffy Williams
Arthur Willimott
Sonny Wilson

MIDLANDS
Reg Airey
George Allbrook
Ivan Anslow
Bill Ashcroft
Stan Baines
Gordon Baxter
Alec Bowerman
Charlie Bowers
Len Bown
Ed Bradley
George Britt
Rocky Burnham
Norman Burton
Les Childer
G.W. Clow
Tom Cross
Les Dallimore
Joe Dallison
Leo Davies
Les Davies
Tommy Deadman
John Deeley
Bill Delaney
George Dykes

Billy Ellmore
Wilmot Evans
Tom Farndon
Jimmy Gent
Dilly Gittins
Joe Gooding
Len Greenhalgh
Joe Hassall
Smiler Henstock
Hal Herbert
Wally Humphrey
Reg Hutchings
Syd Jackson
Arthur Johnson
Nobby Kendrick
Lew Lancaster
Geoff Litherland
Jack Lloyd
Wally Lloyd
Cyril Locke
Cyril Lord
Reg Lucas
Tom McDonald
G. S. Marsh
Jack Parker
Norman Parker
Les Patrick
Bert Perrigo
Bill Pitcher
George Povey
Roy Reeves
Tim Reid
Arthur Sanders
Arthur Sheene
Charlie Shelton
Arthur Sherlock
Slider Shuttleworth
Geoff Siddaway
Cyclone Smith
Bill Stanley
Stan Stannett
Fred Strecker
Cyril Taft
Harry Taft
W. Tandy
Arthur Tims
Arthur Westwood
Nev Wheeler
Bunny Wilcox
Al Wilkinson
Fred Wilkinson

NORTH
Joe Abbott
Bob Allen
Indian Allen
Tommy Allott
Arthur Atkinson
Dennis Atkinson
Jack Atkinson

44

Dick Bailey
Jack Barber
Charlie Barrett
Roy Barrowclough
Clem Beckett
Bronco Bianchi
E. O. Blacknall
Eric Blain
Phil Blake
Billy Blincoe
Len Blunt
Larry Boulton
Buster Breaks
Johnny Broughton
Billy Brown
Dan Buck
Tommy Bullus
Eric Burnet
Frank Burgess
Ham Burrill
Billy Burrows
Squib Burton
Gordon Byers
Jim Cashmore
Arnie Cattell
George Chance
Joe Chance
Jack Chapman
Frank Charles
Frank Chiswell
Jack Chiswell
George Corney
Fred Creasor
Walter Creasor
Monty Cumming
Billy Dallison
Cal Danby
Fred Davenport
Norman Dawson
Paddy Dean
Bronco Dixon
Acorn Dobson
A. B. Drew
Jack Dudding
Ralston Dunlop
Percy Dunn
Ron Durkin
Ted Egerton
Norman Evans
Dick Fletcher
Speed Formby
Arthur Franklyn
Billy Galloway
Tommy Gamble
Harrison Gill
George Greenwood
H. Gresty
N. H. Griffiths
Dusty Haigh
Bob Harrison

Yank Harrison
Norman Hartley
Hurricane Harvey
Tommy Hatch
Dick Hayman
George Hazard
Sid Higgins
Ben Higginbotham
Alec Hill
Charlie Hornby
B. Howard
Chris Hughes
Wally Hull
Austin Humphries
Crazy Hutchins
E. Ingham
Norrie Isbister
Alec Jackson
Dusty Jenkins
Arthur Jervis
Hugh Jervis
Andy Kelly
Geoff Kilburn
Rex Kirby
Skid Knock
Eric Langton
Oliver Langton
Fred Ledger
Johnny Leete
Ginger Lees
W. Lewty
Tommy Lindley
Bill Llewellyn
Johnny Lund
Billy Lye
Wilf McClure
Keith McKay
George McKenzie
Drew M'Queen
R. Marshall
Tommy Mason
Geoff Meredith
Scott Michie
Ken Miller
George Milton
Tom Middlehurst
Joe Mitchell
Chun Moore
Arnold Moore
Alec Moser
Wilf Mulliner
Eddie Myerscough
Len Myerscough
Sid Newiss
Andy Nicoll
Jack Owen
Jack Parsons
Syd Parsons
Alec Peel
Gus Platts

Skid Plevin
Tommy Price
Bud Proctor
Sam Reid
George Reynard
Winks Rice
Riskit Riley
Ian Ritchings
Smoke Robinson
Bert Round
Jack Rowley
Claude Rye
Percy Rye
Stewie St. George
Tiger Sanderson
Jack Scatcherd
Mark Sheldon
W. F. Shuker
Charlie Simpson
Skid Skinner
Ernie Smith
Frank Smith
H. Soloman
Rol Stobart
Tommy Storey
Spencer Stratton
Bill Styring
Bud Thompson
Ron Thompson
Tommy Thompson
Charlie Tobin
Jimmy Valente
Frank Varey
Tommy Wainwright
C. Ward
A. J. Ward
Cliff Watson
Harry Watson
Cliff Whatley
Terry White
George Wigfield
Arthur Wilcock
Cyril Wilcock
Alfie Williams
Freddie Williams
Dick Wise
Johnnie Wood
Jack Woods
Eric Worswick
Leslie Wotton

Riders are listed under the
area in which they were based.

45

The most popular rider of them all?
The 'Cyclone' himself, Billy Lamont

Wally Hull does a wheelie – 1930's
style (Daily Mirror)

Northern pioneer Arnold Moore (C.F. Wallace)

Triss Sharp the Crystal Palace team's first captain

The unmistakable style of Australian rider Max Grosskreutz

Reg Bounds (Wembley Photo)

Nobby Key

Hal Herbert on the old Leicester Super Track (G.A. Shore)

A couple of legendary old timers – Clem Beckett and Stewie St. George

Roger Frogley (T.H. Everitt)

Rol Stobart (centre) in action at Barrow during 1930 (British Photo Press)

Joe Dallison, an early Brummie favourite who rode in their first league match

This photograph of Jack Parker on a 1927 BSA was taken just before he commenced his fabulous career

5

The first touring team

Although Ole Olsen's exploits have put Denmark very much on the modern speedway map, this little European country has been staging the sport for much longer than many people realise. In fact from Morian Hansen and Engstroem to Ole and Finn Thomsen represents a period of nearly fifty years.

It is an interesting fact that a tour, which it is believed was the first to be made by a British team, took place in 1928, when eight men crossed the North Sea to ride in Copenhagen. The team signed up from England consisted of well-known Northern riders Dick Hayman, Ted Egerton and Mark Sheldon, Arthur Greenwood, a works rider from Brough, Ernie Greenall from Oldham, John Crump who manufactured New Henley motor cycles plus Australian star Keith McKay and New Zealander Stewie St. George. A first page of the memorandum of agreement drawn up by the Denmark Track Racing Co. and dated 1st October 1928, is reproduced.

TED EGERTON fills in a few details of the tour. "We sailed from Harwich to Ebjsberg in early October and the Company paid all our travelling expenses, both in England and Denmark. In addition, we were guaranteed £10 per week plus board and lodging and of course retained all prize money won on the track. The only thing that we had to provide was our own machine, but this was maintained and insured at the Company's expense. As you can imagine, with not too many worries we had a lot of fun and did pretty well to start off with, although one or two of the locals, notably Morian Hansen, soon improved rapidly. The tour was such a success that arrangements were made for further excursions in which the top stars like Elder and Lamont took part. It was during one of these later trips that poor Ernie Greenall was killed in a track crash at Copenhagen."

The track at Copenhagen

Memorandum of Agreement made the *first* day of *October* One thousand nine hundred and twenty-*eight* BETWEEN DENMARK TRACK RACING COMPANY LIMITED (a Company incorporated under the Companies Acts 1908 to 1917) whose Registered Office is situate at 3 York Street in the City of Manchester (hereinafter called "the Company") of the one part and *William Edward Egerton, 4 & 6 Knotts Lane, Colne, Track Rider*

(hereinafter called "the Rider") of the other part

WITNESSETH as follows :—

1. THE Rider shall serve the Company as a professional rider on the Company's Dirt Track in Copenhagen aforesaid or any other of the Company's Dirt Tracks from the *Eighth* day of *October 1928* to the *Thirty first* day of *December 1928* or such earlier date (not being less than one month from the said *Eighth* day of *October 1928*) as the weather conditions shall necessitate the closing of the Track which shall be at the sole discretion of the Company

2. DURING the said period from the *Eighth* day of *October 1928* to the *Thirty first* day of *December 1928* the Rider shall not ride for any other Company or firm or on any other Track in Denmark without the written consent of the Company's Managing Director

3. THE Rider shall if required appear and ride at every meeting held on the Company's Track in Copenhagen unless prevented by injury or sickness and also at such other meetings in Denmark as the Company shall determine and the Rider shall in any event be entitled to appear at least *twice per week* during the period for which he is engaged

4. THE Rider shall when required by the Company advise and teach such amateur track riders as may be practising and training in Dirt Track

The front page of the Memorandum of Agreement made when the first touring team visited Denmark during 1928

Copenhagen in 1928. Left to right Stewie St. George, Dick Hayman, Ted Egerton, and Ernie Greenall

6

The forgotten test match

Speedway test matches and internationals have always attracted a great deal of attention and of course, a fair amount of publicity, although newspapers do not perhaps give such extensive coverage today as they did in the past. Nevertheless, England's clashes with other countries are probably the most important events in the British speedway calendar, leaving aside the World's Championship Final, and are guaranteed to at least double normal attendances. Most people are aware of the very first official test match against the Australians, which filled Wimbledon Stadium to its limits and about which so much has been written, but a previous battle between the two countries took place at Brandon, Coventry in September 1929 – a fact which is relatively unknown and in any case seems to have been largely forgotten. This event, put on by the Brandon management with considerable ingenuity and heralded by a blaze of publicity, brought forth a mammoth crowd and produced a whole batch of pre-meeting headaches. Jack Parker, who was a member of the English side on that occasion, has some vivid memories of this astonishing evening, which remain indelibly sketched on his mind.

"This was really the brainchild of Capt. Peacocke, a leading light in the Brandon set-up, and produced a crowd of about 25,000, all of whom somehow or other crammed into the Stadium, which incidentally, was reckoned to have a capacity of less than 10,000! Then when the gates were eventually shut, another 1,000 or so who were locked out swarmed forward, broke down the barriers by the pits and forced an entrance that way, which caused a breakage in the pits electric lighting system. Thus the riders were forced to move themselves and their bikes into the centre of the track. I have never seen anything like it and later on that evening when people were struggling to leave the Stadium, part of the riders' dressing room, which was a wooden structure, was pushed down. Some of the riders trying to take baths were at one time mixed up with spectators!"

However, to the match. For this four-a-side contest, England tracked two local men, Jack Parker and Wilmot Evans, Arthur Jervis from White City, Manchester and Sid Jackson from Leicester whilst the Australian team comprised Frank Arthur, Max Grosskreutz, Col Stewart and the mercurial Billy Lamont. The whole event consisted of a series of two-man match races over 16 heats, with one point awarded for a win. The result was a triumph for the home country by 9½ points to 6½, the half point resulting from a dead-heat between Wilmot Evans and the Southampton Aussie Col Stewart, who later became a Wembley Lion. Top men for the English team were Arthur Jervis and Jack Parker, with three wins each and Jack was credited with the fastest time of the evening – 75 seconds. Wilmot Evans totalled two wins plus that half point and Sid Jackson chalked up a solitary victory. Skipper Frank Arthur was the pick of the visitors and his race with Parker was the tit-bit of the evening. All unofficial of course, but an encounter that certainly had all Coventry buzzing for a long, long time after the dust (and the rubble!) had settled.

The England team prior to the England versus Australia meeting at Belle Vue in 1931. Left to right, Jack Parker, Fred Wilkinson, Eric Langton (Captain), Arthur Franklyn, Ginger Lees, Tommy Croombs, Joe Abbott, Colin Watson, Dusty Haigh, and Frank Varey

Practising at the Sydney Royale track during England's first official tour of Australia. Note the dust
(The Sun, Australia)

54

7

Jack Barnett-part-time champion

JACK BARNETT's place in speedway history is assured, even if only for the fact that he was one of the tiny band of what could fairly be described as amateur riders and was certainly the most successful of this exclusive group. If proof of this is needed, Jack was the first acknowledged Champion of our first track High Beech, which has been in most people's thoughts during the last year or so and he received more trophies from the hands of celebrities than anyone I can remember! In between his many present day pursuits, which include gliding, Jack was reliving some of his adventures in those hazy, crazy days down at Kings Oak.

"Most of my riding was done at High Beech where I held the records during 1929 but had my nose put out of joint by Phil Bishop who came along in 1930 and took them from me. In those days, we used to have a rolling start when, in theory, all riders crossed the line at the same time. I say in theory because it was possible to get your throttle wide open a moment before any of the others and so cross the line at the same time but going somewhat faster! This of course, didn't always come off; I remember a match race I had with Billy Lamont when he had a very hot AJS. We went over the line together but when I got round the first bend, Bill was at the far end of the straight! But I won the race because of a happening I have never seen before or since – his back wheel came out of the frame, and shot up into the air about ten feet, but he didn't fall off – just slid to a stop with both feet firmly on the ground! I also remember Billy riding at Exeter one time. The track in those days had a very high banking with a wooden track between the cinders and the fence. Not content with riding up the banking, Bill rode up the wooden track and then on to the fence and ripped off the sole of his boot. This didn't affect him in the least – he just ploughed on and won his race as usual.

I was one of a small band of riders who kept a daytime job and turned out on tracks all over the country in the evenings or when I had taken a day off from work. I used to go to Exeter quite often. This entailed having an afternoon off, taking a couple of bikes by car to Paddington and putting them and us on the train to Exeter. The first time that we went to Devon, the natives made a polite enquiry – were we returning on the midnight train? We supposed so and duly made our way to the station to discover that the midnight train left Exeter at 2 a.m. We used to have a sleeper, pick up the bikes at Paddington and be home in time to get to the office. Another time, I was booked to ride at Nottingham at 7.30 one evening and was unable to get time off. So my bikes went up by car during the day and I arranged to fly – I was the office boy in those days (!) and left the office at 5 pm on my TT Sunbeam arriving at Stag Lane at 5.30. The plane was standing warming up; I signed an indemnity absolving the air taxi service of any liability no matter what they did to me and we took off at a quarter to six. We landed at Nottingham at six forty-five; a car was waiting and we were at the Stadium by seven o'clock. I thought that two hours door to door in those days wasn't bad going.

One of my more embarrassing moments was when I won the Golden Gauntlet at West Ham. I reached the final with Sprouts Elder and Roger Frogley. After the first lap I was last, then I saw Roger at the side of the track and realised I was second – another lap and there was Sprouts broken down which left me first! I had to ride a lap of honour wearing the Gauntlet and as I was the local boy made good, the spectators swarmed all over the greyhound track and there seemed to be millions wishing me well. On the other hand, a very gratifying moment occurred at the 40 years celebration at High Beech in 1968. A supporter from Manchester approached me and asked 'Are you Jack Barnett?' He had with him a size-able album – it looked about one foot long and two feet wide, full of cigarette pictures. He asked me it I

Syd Edmonds (left) and Jack Barnett fight for the lead at High Beech (Harold White)

Jack Barnett's mode of transport in 1929

would autograph the one of myself which I did with great pleasure, seeing that he had waited forty years to catch up with me!"

Before we leave Jack, perhaps we could mention his 'twin' SYD EDMONDS, who skippered the High Beech side in the days when Jack was burning up the cinders and taking on all comers at the 'Forest'. Syd, a great spectacle merchant, had many a friendly battle with Jack and headed a team which included another thrill-a-minute man, Phil Bishop and crowd pleasers Billy Dallison and Bobby Blake – this all added up to a combination worth travelling miles to see. Syd, one of the nicest guys in the game, knew and got on well with all the early Australians, but the one that he mentions with particular affection is Bluey Wilkinson. "He was the greatest" says Syd.

58

8

Wal Phillips – what an experience

To some, certain events in those far off days of 1929 are hard to recall, but I asked WAL PHILLIPS, famous English International, Brooklands star and mechanical genius who was selected for the first English team to do battle with the Australians, if he remembered anything of his very first speedway meeting at the legendary Stamford Bridge track. I found that he not only remembered it, but each race is still clear in his mind.

"Oh, yes I can tell you quite a bit about my first speedway meeting. I got to Stamford Bridge a long time before racing was due to commence and had a cup of tea in the little cafe whilst I watched the other riders arrive and warm up their machines. I was in no hurry as I had travelled to the track in my leathers and quite frankly, there was no point in warming up my Scott - it was so worn out that it made no difference whether it started hot or cold! I wasn't even nervous as I had no thoughts of winning anything on the old bike and regarded this simply as extra practice.

Suddenly I was in the Grand Parade which opened the evening and it was then that I noticed the enormous crowd and quite a few butterflies started to come to life in my stomach! I began to wonder – supposing my performance was so poor that they booed me or even threw things! I then discovered from the programme that my first heat contained Gus Kuhn, a top class motorcyclist with a tremendous reputation and who in fact had beaten me in a road race at Crystal Palace fairly recently. However, I noticed that I was to receive 25 yards start, which made me feel a bit better and determined to have a go. There were two other boys in the race both on 15 yards and Gus of course started from scratch.

The starter's gun sounded and my Scott fired at once. I leaped into the saddle, rode into the first corner and completed one lap shutting off for a moment on entering the corners or if I overdid a slide. I reached the third lap still in front and thoughts of winning entered my mind but then with a roar Gus Kuhn flashed by me as if I were standing still! He pulled over to the line but I continued on my course half way up the banking and to my astonishment caught Gus again in the middle of the next corner. However, on the next straight he was away again– he seemed to have so much speed it just wasn't true, but having caught him once, I had the bit between my teeth and decided it was neck or nothing. I shot into the next bend far too recklessly without shutting off but somehow held it and came out level with him and on the next corner actually got my nose in front. With one more turn, I thought that I must have a chance but by the time I had reached it Gus had once more gained a two lengths lead. I tore into this last bend flat out, went by him, skidded out to the fence, bumped against the wire and headed for the finishing line – then another roar and Gus was up there with me and about a length clear at the flag!

Almost before I could get my breath back in the pits, it was the semi-final of the Handicap event and a repetition of our heat as Gus repeated his win over me but again I came second and therefore qualified for the final. I suddenly became nervous again but calmed down and made a perfect start. I entered the first bend flat out and overslid but managed to stay in the saddle. On the next corner I went out too far and hit the fence with a mighty wallop – miraculously, I controlled the bike but refused to shut the throttle as I knew old Gus was beginning to breathe down my neck. The track was getting bumpy and the Scott was occasionally taking-off but I knew that I must not relax for a moment. Then the inevitable happened and by the time we had finished the second lap, Gus had taken the lead. In desperation, I decided to ride a different course, cutting in close to the corner wishing all the time that I had a little more speed. By this time we were at the end of the third lap and I was still two or three lengths adrift. I rode that last lap like something possessed and almost had him on the last straight but Gus was still a whisker ahead as we

Wal Phillips

Wal Phillips in action

60

entered the final bend. It was all or nothing, I went up the banking full throttle and edged past Gus on the outside trying to keep from tangling with the fence. I got my head down and went for the finishing line but there was Gus, that master of throttle control, up beside me and using his extra speed to pip me on the post!

We shook hands and I drifted back to the pits a little disconsolately, then noticed a peculiar roaring sound and as I stopped, I heard the crowd shouting 'We want Phillips' repeating it over and over again and the announcer was powerless to quieten them and unable to continue. Promoter Claude Langdon ran over to me 'Get out there and give an exhibition of broadsiding – anything'. I was so dumbfounded, I just went out and rode and trying to pull out something extra, fell twice, got up and went on to complete five laps before returning to the pits. The vast crowd was still making a deafening noise and Langdon told me that as a bonus, I was being given a match race with Doug Wilson, whom I managed to beat narrowly.

My reward for the evening was to go to the Royal Box where famous racing motorist Kaye Don presented me with an envelope and on the way, people were slapping me on the back and wishing me well – it is something that I could never forget. When I eventually did get away somewhere quiet, I opened the envelope and found £12.10s which was more than I had ever possessed before. So you can see why I remember my first meeting so very vividly".

The first World Champion – Lionel Van Praag

9

Tommy Price – World Champion

It must be a marvellous experience to be proclaimed Speedway Champion of the World especially if you are an English World Champion – after all up until 1979, only three men had achieved this honour. I asked TOMMY PRICE the first Englishman to win the crown, what it felt like and to relate some of the events that led up to it.

"Obviously, I felt wonderful" said Tommy, "and in my case it was doubly welcome as I had faced a very worrying time beforehand. For the previous couple of months, I had lost some form and in the qualifying round was drawn at a Second Division track, Newcastle, about which I knew very little. The day before I was due to ride at Brough Park, I had to turn out at Belle Vue, where I fared only moderately, so during that night I worked like mad on my bike and travelled to Newcastle, knowing that everything depended on this particular meeting. Fortunately, I made some good starts and topped the score chart, which put me in good heart. However, there is a story here – when I got back to Wembley, I rode the next meeting with the same engine and in my first race the con-rod broke and the engine blew to bits. If that had happened in my previous ride (the last heat at Newcastle) it is doubtful if I would have qualified for the next round, which all goes to show....

Before the Final, I was pretty confident as I felt I had regained my best form but some people laughed as I took four or five spare wheels as well as two machines to the meeting – I was leaving nothing to chance. I put on a new wheel before every race and only missed the gate once and here I had a little bit of luck. Wilbur Lamoreaux made the first bend in front of me and in trying to pass him, my bike stood up on its back wheel. Before I could right it, Ron Clarke had gone past me too. Then Lammy oiled a plug and I was through and in front of both of them. As I crossed the finishing line, I felt like a million dollars and the past started to flash through my mind – I could remember seeing Jack Parker ride some fabulous races at Wembley and Bill Kitchen putting up some marvellous performances on his visits with Belle Vue – all this before I had ever sat astride a speedway machine. I never thought at that time that I would ever be emulating their feats, let alone become World Champion.

Unfortunately, there was a little bit of feeling after the meeting was over because I didn't attend the reception, and I'll tell you the reason. About a week before the final, Harringay's George Kay had come up to me and said 'We think you could possibly win the Final and so would you turn out in a prestige meeting at Harringay on the following night' to which I agreed. However, after my Wembley win, I knew that there were some who regarded my success as a little fortunate and I reasoned that if I stayed late at the reception and had a few drinks etc. I might not be perfectly fit for the following evening. After all, it would be my first meeting as World Champion and everyone would be watching to see whether my win was just a flash in the pan; I was determined to do myself justice. As it happens, I went through the Harringay meeting undefeated so in a way, I felt justified. Looking back though, I wish now that I had attended the reception as I upset a few people, including Sir Arthur Elvin for whom I had a great regard, but it was not meant in any way as a snub.

On the subject of the World Championship, I got nearly as big a kick eleven years earlier when, in 1938, I qualified for the World Final whilst only a reserve for the Wembley Lions. This was, of course, Bluey's year, and although I didn't get anywhere in the actual placings, you can imagine what a thrill it was riding against Jack Milne, Lamoreaux, Jack Parker, Eric Langton, Van Praag, George Newton and others of such standing".

1978 Golden Jubilee Year World Champion
and Captain of the League Championship
winners, Coventry – Ole Olsen, one of the
all-time greats

64

Tommy Price, the successful team manager with the 1965 league champions – West Ham

Tommy Price in action at a wartime Belle Vue meeting

Tommy, a product of the old Barnet grass-cum-cinder track, had trials for Harringay before Wembley took him on and in those days was a great fan of Ron Johnson – he reckoned he learned lots from the Australian maestro. He speaks with affection too of many of his England colleagues, especially Eric French and Geoff Pymar. It was Geoff who brought the news of the death of his great friend and Wembley colleague, Frank Charles, who was killed in a glider accident – Tommy heard the sad news one night whilst he was riding at Belle Vue and strangely, he had a premonition just before Geoff arrived in the pits.

Tom is still very interested in the modern speedway scene – after all, it is not such a long time since he team managed West Ham to their first British League Championship win. He well remembers giving a first outing to a youngster by the name of Malcolm Simmons.

'Pip' Price in action at Cardiff during 1929

10

Speedway in Wales

For one reason or another, speedway racing has invariably had a struggle to capture the imagination of the Welsh people. Many tracks have tried their luck over the years but few have flourished – some have opened their doors with great hopes only to succumb after a matter of months. Amongst those attempting to establish speedway in the Principality have been the two Cardiff tracks, one at Tredegar where ambitious colliers built a circuit of their own on the hilly slopes of the mining village, Pontypridd, Caerphilly and more recently, the brief ill-fated venture at Neath. A year ago Newport had to give up the struggle, although one hopes that this will be only a temporary set-back. Even as I write, there is a possibility that Cardiff may soon be staging racing once more. However, back to the early days when former Welsh Champion IVOR HILL has some interesting stories to tell of those pioneering times.

"I started on the old Sloper Road circuit in Cardiff in 1929, which was managed by Jimmy Hindle, who also rode in addition to his managerial duties. In my first season mounted on a Douglas, I won the Golden Helmet three times and was consequently asked to ride a Scott at Pontypridd and at the same time, make an attempt on the track record. I was going great guns until the left handlebar grip came off in my hand and I went over the top, ending up with concussion. That was the finish of the Scott as far as I was concerned! I remember well my first Duggie which was delivered to me at Sloper Road and I thought I would give it a trial run. In those days, the front spindle was slotted into the forks but unfortunately the front wheel came out of the forks whilst I was in the middle of a slide, with the result that I finished up with the bike on my back, the engine still running. A couple of seasons after I commenced racing, I was chosen as a member of the Welsh speedway team which rode against Wembley at the Empire Stadium. In our team that day was Len Parker, an official rider for Douglas. It was he, I believe, who introduced the heavy studded rear tyre which is in general use today and we turned up at Wembley where we soundly defeated the home side. This made Johnnie Hoskins, who was running the track at the time, very annoyed because he said that these big rear tyres of ours had thrown all the cinders off his track onto the dog track! I recall too, the legendary Sprouts Elder being invited to Cardiff and using a special fuel of his own which smelt like boot polish!

Digressing from Wales for a moment, an outstanding memory is of the time when riders used to turn out on what is known in dog circles as 'flapping tracks' using assumed names. One such track was at Norwich and as I remember, my name there was 'Wally Bird'. As far as I know, no one ever discovered 'Wally's' true identify! Then there was the classic time when the promoters let the bookmakers in to a certain stadium and they began to make a book on the races. Needless to say, this was an opportunity too good to miss and we had a brother of one of the riders up in the stands putting on the bets whilst we organised the races. I need hardly say that they never came again to make a book on speedway racing!

We had our share of problems with machines – in those early days a fall would sometimes cause cinders to clog the chain and there could be great difficulty in wheeling the bike afterwards, the chain being full of cinders. The added strain also tended to twist the frame. One rider got over this problem by completely reversing everything, turning his engine round so that the primary chain, countershaft and rear chain were all on the offside of the machine instead of the nearside. This required a fair amount of technical ability as the engine had to be converted to run in the opposite direction to which it was designed to run, otherwise the bike would have gone backwards!

One or two of the early tracks were unorthodox to say the least of it, and I have rather a painful memory of one of them, Stamford Bridge, before it underwent substantial alterations. It was at that time

69

Ivor Hill flat out

The Welsh team that defeated Wembley in 1929. Ivor Hill, 'Hurricane' Hampson, Ronnie Baker, Jimmy Hindle, 'Champ' Upham, Jack Luke, and A. N. Other (Photopress)

Cardiff's opening meeting on Boxing Day 1928. Rider on the left is 'Pip' Price on an AJS

Cardiff 1929 – Dell Forster, Ivor Hill, Nobby Key and Nick Carter

most unusual, consisting of two long straights and two banked bends and called for a rather special riding technique different from the normal oval circuits – the method employed was to ride up to the apex of each bend, do a quick turn and ride down again! The visiting riders, who were accustomed to the more orthodox method of broadsiding round each bend, might get to the corner first but would be passed by a home rider swooping off the banking and going past at a great rate of knots, sometimes resulting in accidents. One day when Wimbledon were visiting, Claude Rye and Ted Bravery were lying in Hammersmith Hospital betting who would be the next victim – unfortunately it happened to be me with a broken wrist and a nasty cut on my face, the scar of which I carry to this day."

Despite these setbacks, Ivor had a colourful career which included visits to South Africa and Australia, where he toured with the English team at the same time as the famous and controversial cricket 'bodyline' tour featuring Harold Larwood. He rode league speedway for several years with Harringay, Wimbledon and Nottingham before further injuries prompted him to call it a day. Ivor's main interests these days are golf and his business near Wimbledon Stadium, where he is a main Lancia dealer.

Another Welsh pioneer is 'PIP' PRICE. Domiciled in Bridgend, he signed for the Cardiff track at dinner in Barry's Hotel in October 1928 and made his racing debut on Boxing Day of the same year. The following meeting took place in January 1929, complete with frozen cinders, six men taking part in each race, and as there were seven heats, the slowest winner dropped out for the final! As you can imagine, all hell was let loose when this decision was announced!

A Cardiff team was formed in the early part of 1929 and 'Pip' captained the locals until he broke his collar-bone later that year, necessitating a short spell on the sidelines, but he came back to win the Golden Sash and the Golden Helmet. This was the White City's premier honour and was competed for each alternate Saturday, carrying a prize of £10, which was worth winning. 'Pip' remembers with affection some of his colleagues and 'oppos' from those days such as Ronnie Baker, local boy 'Champ' Upham, 17 year old James Douglas, grandson of the founder of Douglas Motors of Bristol, 'Hurricane' Hampson, Jack Luke, Stanley Gill from Bath and a gentleman rejoicing in the name of Baron R. Jenkinson!

Of all these sons of Wales though, none has brought fame to the Land of the Valleys in quite the same way as has FREDDIE WILLIAMS, the man who brought the World Championship to Wales for the first time in 1950 and repeated the feat three years later. Ex-engineering fitter Fred, from Port Talbot, shook the speedway world when he won his first championship, defeating all the more fancied candidates except Jack Parker. Fred's introduction to the Sport was through answering an advertisement in 1945 – this called for men with motorcycling experience (preferably grass track) to come for a try-out at the Rye House training school at Hoddesden. From there Fred graduated to the Wembley league side and gained many International caps as well as his two World titles.

Before we conclude our brief look at the Welsh scene, I wonder if anyone is aware that an England v Wales contest took place at Wimbledon in 1929? The result was a win for England by 40 points to 23 and home stars Jim Kempster, Eric Spencer and Colin Watson all scored maximum points. For the Welshmen, Len Parker, Nobby Key and Ronnie Baker topped the score chart.

72

11

The Scottish Scene

Soon after the opening of High Beech, the majority of overseas stars arrived in this country and Jimmy Baxter began to look around for a further venue for them to demonstrate their skills. He eventually decided on Celtic Park, Glasgow, and that is where Scotland saw its first properly organised racing with safety fences etc. Scottish speedway folk though were inclined to be a wee bit inconsistent in their support of the bread and butter meetings and with maximum attendances of 5,000 and prize money alone of £400 per meeting to be found, promotional headaches were plentiful! However, one event that has been a winner from the start is the Scottish Championship – in fact, the 1929 Championship staged in Edinburgh attracted no less that thirty-five thousand people, who saw twenty seven riders drawn from Scotland, England, America and Australia battling it out for the country's top honour. It may be of interest to fans north of the border and to others historically minded if I give brief details of this encounter.

The first heat produced a win for local star Drew McQueen from Newcastle's Walter Creasor, whilst James Logie finished up in the fence. Heat two went to Australian Syd Parsons followed by Chris Hughes and Bob McGregor and heat number three to another Aussie Col Stewart who led home Dick Wise and Bill Dickie. The fourth heat caused something of a sensation as the favourite for the title, Sprouts Elder, fell, bringing down Tiger Sanderson from Newcastle. Fortunately, neither was hurt, but it let in Glasgow lad Andy Marr for a surprise win. The fifth and sixth heats again supplied Australian victors in Ned Kelly who beat Sam Reid and Jim Holder and Jack Chapman who disposed of Maurice Bradshaw and Andy Nicoll – the latter taking a rather painful toss. Heat seven was won narrowly by Billy Galloway from local laddie Eric Burnet and O. Goodfellow; Heat eight provided the first English winner in Ivor Creek, who came home ahead of Harry Duncan and George McKenzie, and the last of the qualifying heats went to Norrie Isbister from Andy Milne and Billy Naismith.

In the first semi-final, Drew McQueen beat Syd Parsons and Col Stewart, Ned Kelly took the second semi from Jack Chapman and Andy Marr and Billy Galloway was successful in the third with Ivor Creek and Norrie Isbister following him home. In the Final, amidst scenes of great enthusiasm, Drew McQueen made a fine start and held on to beat Billy Galloway by twenty yards, with Ned Kelly third. Drew was presented with the Scottish Championship trophy, £100 and the SACA Golf Medallion.

One of Scotland's top riders in early times was NORRIE ISBISTER, later to promote at Ashfield. He rubbed shoulders with the men of Celtic Park in '28, names alas long forgotten like Scotsman Ralston Dunlop, James Valente, George Cummings, Graeme Morrison, Bill McLaren, John Walker and more prominent riders who have become part and parcel of Speedway's romantic past. These included popular Drew McQueen, Keith McKay and Geoff Meredith of Australia, Stewie St. George and Spencer Stratton of New Zealand, not forgetting the one and only Sprouts Elder and one of the first Englishmen to cross swords with the rampaging Aussies, Ivor Creek.

I asked Norrie what he remembered of the birth and progress of speedway in Scotland.

"As you know, dirt track came to Scotland in April 1928 at Celtic Park football ground and Scotland's second track opened at Marine Gardens, Edinburgh in June 1928 – to be more correct Portobello, not far from the centre of the city. Yes, you youngsters, I said 'dirt track', we didn't have such a posh name as speedway in those days. And let me assure you that the emphasis was on the 'dirt'.

I wonder how many fans of today realise just where the sport originated in Glasgow? Apart from a few who had heard or read about dirt tracks down under, we didn't have much of a clue so we formed a small club and took over a ground by the name of Nelson Ground, then a pony trotting track with genuine

A 1950 photograph of Ken Le Breton in action (Sport and General Press Agency)

Post-war Glasgow favourite Will Lowther

Ken Le Breton in his famous white leathers

74

Col Stewart

hairpin bends, the surface rock hard and a four foot fence on the INSIDE. Monty Cumming, Jimmy Valente, myself and one or two others ran a few meetings and were quite enjoying it when who should appear in our so called pits but Billy Galloway. He was the carrier of good news – he had arrived from Australia with Keith McKay, Paddy Dean, Buzz Hibberd, Stewie St. George and others. They had taken an office in Howard Street, Glasgow and were presenting Dirt Track Racing at Celtic Park. They were a bit unfortunate and didn't get sufficient public support, so in July they closed.

The poor old pioneers had a hard life and believe me, the show and the organisation was good. We had handicap races (push start) and maybe a match race worth £10 to the winner, scratch races – two in each heat, semi-final and final, worth £37.

Monty Cumming and I moved to Manchester and signed on with the British Dirt Track Riders Association, who promoted this new sport at White City. When the season ended around 14th November, I came home. Monty moved to Sheffield and helped with the birth of the first track in that town and it was one of the best – Owlerton, Frank Varey's first love.

The stars at that time at Celtic Park and Marine Gardens, apart from those already mentioned like Elder, St.George, Stratton etc, were Col Stewart, Hibberd and a little later Frank Arthur, Jack Parker, Billy Lamont, Colin Watson, the Frogley brothers and our own stars from Glasgow and Edinburgh after they had worked their way through the novice stages. Here I must, of course, mention particularly Drew McQueen and George McKenzie.

Having been associated with speedway for so many years, I have met and ridden with countless numbers of riders, but of them all, one name stands out in my memory – that brilliant performer Ken Le Breton who rode for me at Ashfield. Ken would, I am sure, have become World Champion but for that tragic accident which cost him his life."

Although Scottish speedway has had a somewhat chequered history, the sport seems, happily, to have become re-established in Edinburgh and Glasgow during the last year or two. Despite its ups and downs, the country has brought forth many fine riders, amongst them Tommy Miller, Ken McKinlay, Gordon McGregor and Jim McMillan. Mention of Jim links us with present day speedway and who better to bring us up to date with the modern Scottish scene than that colourful character, Bert Harkins, skipper of the revitalised Edinburgh Monarchs, a team which made a most welcome return to the sport in 1977. I asked Bert for some of his own recollections and thoughts on the present situation.

'Well, speedway racing in Scotland has come a long way since the leg-trailing days of Norrie Isbister, Billy Galloway and Co., but many Scots, with long memories, still talk of those halcyon pre-war times when dirt tracking was the name of the game!

The machines have progressed from the Dirt Track Duggies and Peashooter Harleys, through the long-stroke and short-stroke JAPS, to the present 4-valve Weslakes, Jawas and the like.

Charlie Monk in his White City days battles
with the popular 'Wild Man' Vic Lonsdale

76

Scottish favourite of the late 40's, Jack Young, visiting Tommy Bateman after the dreadful crash which ended Tommy's speedway career (Scottish Daily Mail)

Norrie Isbister, the promoter, with his 1951 Ashfield team (J.A.S. Gray)

Bert Harkins

Lined up at the White City, Glasgow, 1929. Riders are Norrie Isbister, A.N. Other, Drew McQueen, Billie Llewellyn, Alfie Williams (Weir)

Track surfaces have changed immensely and are now hard and slick compared with the deep cinders of the pioneers. Riders' equipment has also progressed with the early pudding-basin type of helmet being replaced by the full-face and jet-type of headgear, a major step towards safety in speedway.

But to return to Scottish speedway. It seems that **everyone** was a speedway fan in those pre-war days, and in my home town of Glasgow, folks still talk about the visit of the legendary American, Sprouts Elder, to the old White City circuit.

It seems that the lanky Sprouts came to town and put on a truly spectacular show, overtaking his opponents down the long White City straights with his front wheel high in the air. I guess he was one of the top showmen of the pre-war days and from what I have heard, he had the shrewd business brain to capitalize on his talents on a motorcycle! One report states that he asked for–and received– a £1,000 signing-on fee from Southampton and could earn a few hundred pounds per week from appearance fees alone throughout the country! Those must have been the days.

Pre-war riders like Jack and Cordy Milne and 'Pee-Wee' Cullum were just names in the sport's Hall of Fame history books until I made my first trip over to Los Angeles with my crash helmet tucked under my arm. There I met up with Jack, who was running the tiny Costa Mesa track in Orange County, California, with 'Pee-Wee' in the role of Chief Starting Marshal. Jack still has a huge selection of trophies which he collected during his racing days, but many of those are now stored in cardboard boxes in the garage beside his house!

Jack's most memorable visit to Scotland was back in 1938 when, as World Champion, he was invited to race at Glasgow White City along with brother Cordy and fellow Californian, Wilbur Lamoreaux.

Promoter Johnnie Hoskins had invited Sir Harry Lauder along as guest of honour and he sat in the grandstand alongside Mr. Milne senior, father of Cordy and Jack. When Sir Harry made the trophy presentation to Jack Milne, he mentioned that, as the World Champion's father was a Scot from Aberdeen, perhaps Jack and Cordy would be eligible to ride for Scotland in their next Speedway International against the "Auld Enemy",....England! I'll bet the patriotic Scots fans loved that piece of news!

Now, with speedway racing in this country having passed its 50th Anniversary, the fans North of the border are just as patriotic and enthusiastic as ever. Way back in April 1928, a Mr. James Baxter opened Glasgow Celtic's football stadium for the new sport of speedway racing and the future of Scottish Speedway is looking very healthy.

In April 1977 the return of the sport to the nation's capital city, Edinburgh, was a tremendous shot in the arm, and with the successful transfer of the Tigers from Coatbridge to Blantyre, we now have two of the clubs with the longest histories in action again,....Edinburgh Monarchs and Glasgow Tigers.

It was as a Glasgow Tigers' supporter that I first caught the speedway bug when my father used to take me along to the old White City track and perch me on his shoulders to catch a glimpse of my heroes, Junior Bainbridge, Tommy Miller and Ken McKinlay. The bug stayed with me and, when I was eventually able to buy a speedway machine....an ancient JAP cost me all of £40. The only speedway track in Scotland at that time was Edinburgh, some 50 miles away.

Rides were hard to get and, with about 20 or 30 novices lining up all hoping to get a few laps at the end of the meeting, you can guess that there was not much opportunity of making progress even to reserve standard. It was a case of travelling through to Edinburgh (often on an old motorcycle with my speedway JAP tied onto the sidecar chassis!) and hoping to be allowed onto the track at the end of the official programme. If you were unlucky, you just had to head off home and try again the following week.

Recently, we have had the excellent Scottish Junior League with teams from Edinburgh, Glasgow, Berwick and the now defunct Paisley Lions. The latter Junior team was sponsored by the ever-loyal Paisley Supporters Club.

The idea was the brain-child of Dick Barrie who did a great job at getting the League off the ground. So much so, that Junior teams South of the border queued up to compete against the young Scots. It is a great way of giving a junior that extra experience he needs to make the grade, much better than having only one race per week for the juniors. It also gives the new novices something to aim for, as a place in the Junior League squad is the first stepping stone to a full team place.

Yes, you can safely say that the future of speedway in Scotland looks brighter than it has for a long, long time and whilst there are people and promoters within the sport who will help the novices, the blue and white cross of Saint Andrew will continue to flourish in International competitions in the years to come. We may not legtrail like the stars of yesteryear, but the sheer enthusiasm which surrounds the sport in the Land O' the Heather, will keep the fans, riders and promoters happy until speedway's 100th anniversary!'.

12

Argentina and Frank Varey

I suppose that if the man in the street who knew little about speedway was invited to name six riders or personalities connected with sport, it is a fair bet, particularly if he happened to be a Northerner, that one of the names would be FRANK VAREY. Rider, promoter, track expert, character extraordinary he was at one time the most controversial performer in the game.

Apart from his successful riding career in England, which earned him many international caps, the best known of his exploits occurred in Argentina during the early thirties. It was here that his famous Scott with the high pitched exhaust 'yowl' and its red frame and red tank coupled with his red jersey earned him the name of El Diablo Rojo (The Red Devil) by which he is still known.

"Yes", says Frank, "we had a lot of adventures and a lot of fun in Buenos Aires, but it was not always so pleasant. One year we went out to Montevideo following a request from the promoters to take some secondhand speedway bikes to sell to the locals and at the same time do a bit of riding. So we got together a team of six, but on arrival found that the track was still under construction and we had to wait for about three weeks before we could ride. Once we got going, Eric Langton and I cleaned up most of the prize money as there was not a lot of competition, but the selling of the bikes was a different matter – we had to use the hire purchase system and it was some job getting the instalments when they were due!

Towards the end of December, things went from bad to worse financially, as the speedway company went broke so Eric Langton and I slipped across the river to Buenos Aires to see whether we could get speedway going there again. Anyhow, we got everything fixed up beautifully and caught the night boat back to Montevideo to tell the other lads the good news, but when we arrived they were running about with newspapers shouting something about a speedway rider being killed. We then discovered that Bob Harrison and Clem Cort had been involved in an accident, and Clem had died after being taken to hospital. To make things even worse, when the police discovered that Bob had been driving they clapped him in jail. We had to put our hands deep into our pockets to find the money to buy a bit of land to bury poor Clem and after the funeral, we got Bob out on bail and jumped on the next boat for the Argentine.

For our first meeting in Buenos Aires, we hit on the idea of a benefit for Mrs Cort, but it rained all day and all night which put paid to that. Eventually we did get it under way and had a bumper crowd, which made enough money to get Mrs Cort home to Australia and at the same time put a little into our own pockets, for by that time we were skint! By and large though, Buenos Aires was great, although there was another year when the speedways went bust out there. The owner, Jack Nelson, agreed to pay our fares back to England but he got stuck in the wilds and couldn't return for some time, so I wired Belle Vue to say would they please pay our fares so that we could get back to Manchester. In those days it was only £39 apiece. A few days later back came the reply from E.O. Spence – 'SWIM'. I can just imagine a rider getting that sort of reply today! However, to start off with we saw the funny side of it, although by the time we arrived home, having paid our own fares, we were pretty angry and thought we would show the Belle Vue management what we thought of them. We were determined to make the next meeting an absolute farce, but instead of doing what we intended, I was the fool who went out in the first race and broke the track record! E.O. Spence came up to me afterwards and said 'I knew you would do that tonight, Frank!' He was a very wily old bird was E.O., one of the shrewdest promoters we have ever had."

I asked Frank about his appearance in the first test match. "Naturally, I was very proud to be chosen for the very first test and really looking forward to it as I was cleaning up at a number of Northern tracks but a shock was in store. I had never seen Wimbledon before in my life – I had been used to flat out tracks and hadn't a clue how to ride such a tricky circuit. My mechanic and I couldn't agree about the gearing

81

Frank Varey on the Buenos Aires track

Clem Court

82

Another view of the Buenos Aires track. Note the long straight

The first bend – Buenos Aires in the early 1930's

Two aces: The first Belle Vue champion poses with the present No. 1 – Frank Varey and Peter Collins

84

Members of the touring team at the Huracan Speedway 1929. Left to right, Pug McCullum, Buzz Hibberd, Ivor Creek, Jack Harris, Sprouts Elder, Frank Duckett, Eric Langton, Max Grosskreutz, Oliver Langton, Hugh Jervis, Bob Harrison, Roberto Sigrand, Dusty Haigh, George Corney, Sid Newiss, and Dank Ewin

and we finished up with the wrong gear and wrong everything – in short I was a bit of a flop! On the way home I told my mechanic that I was done for and would have to think of retiring, but he soon talked me out of that. One strange thing happened at a test match a couple of years later. It was at Stamford Bridge, where I loved to ride, and in an early heat I crashed rather badly and was carried off unconscious. Almost immediately all the lights around the track went out! Everybody lit newspapers and bonfires around the ground and it must have been quite a sight although I wasn't in a position to see. Anyway they got the power working again and the announcer told the crowd that I wouldn't be riding in my next heat but I had come round by then and heard the announcement from the ambulance room. I was out of the door in a flash and just to prove that I was OK, I jumped on my bike, joined the others at the starting line and managed to win the race."

Frank Varey's partnership with Eric Langton at Belle Vue reaped a harvest of points for club and country and is one of the most famous duos in the Sport's history. In fact, they were both chosen as members of the first official English team to visit Australia for a series of test matches.

Frank made a come-back last year by doing a few laps on his old Scott machine at Belle Vue's Golden Jubilee meeting, much to the delight of the crowd and photographers alike. Needless to say, he avoided letting his wife know beforehand!

Keith Harvey – the first South African to make his mark

13

Speedway in South Africa

I am sure that most of us would jump at the chance of a trip to South Africa but for IVOR HILL that controversial country holds mixed memories – pleasant and very much otherwise! Ivor was chosen as a member of the English speedway team which went over in 1930, to race a series of test matches against the home country. Here is his story.

"This was my first visit to Africa and on arrival we had problems with the tuning of the bikes. Because Jonannesburg is so far above sea level the atmosphere becomes a bit rare and it completely upset the carburation, so I decided to run my bike on dope (in those days quite a lot of machines were still on petrol or benzole.) I went to a firm of manufacturing chemists who agreed to make me up a fuel on which I could run my engine on high compression — I can remember the formula to this day, it was 75% methylated spirit, 20% benzine, 3% acetone and 2% ether. I ran this on about a 9 : 1 compression ratio and managed to get the bike going pretty quickly, so much so that at one of the meetings at Krugersdorp, I loaned it to Wally Lloyd who broke the track record on it.

However, reverting to the tests, on the evening of the first test match at Ellis Park, just before the racing was due to start, and with the stadium filled, the home riders went on strike, demanding more money for their services. For some reason unknown to us, the SA public blamed the English boys and the situation looked decidedly sticky but ultimately, the promoters acceded to the South African riders' request and the meeting went on. By this time, the Englishmen were so incensed that they decided to do 'em in no uncertain manner – the result was a win for us by 37 points to 17 and I finished the evening with the track record. The promoters were so upset by this that they refused to run any more meetings, so there we were in Africa with no means of earning our living. We therefore approached the promoters and they agreed that we could rent the track and organise our own meetings. As we could not afford to employ labour, we prepared the track ourselves and invited the SA riders to race against us, taking good care to put two English boys in each race with two Africans so that we did not have to pay out too much prize money! Things went very well except that due to our inexperience and no doubt our youth, we omitted to advise the public transport authorities that we were running that night and consequently there were thousands of people who were unable to get to the stadium as it was some way from Jo'burg to the Cindrena. However, we made a modest profit from the evening and decided that since we had more than our fill, the best thing would be to make our way back home. In the meantime, I received a bill from a freight company for the transport of my Rudge machine from England, together with Nobby Key's. The reason for this was that when we undertook to go to South Africa, we were told to bring Douglas machines with us as they were more spectacular, but on arrival we found that the home riders were mounted on Rudges, which put us at a distinct disadvantage! So I trotted along to this freight firm and asked them to bring Nobby Key's Rudge and my own to Johannesburg. When the bill eventually arrived (which was **after** the closure of the track by the promoters) I went along to a local firm of solicitors, who advised me not to pay as it was the responsibility of the promoters. Unfortunately, they didn't see it like that and when I arrived at the booking office to collect tickets for a trip to Durban, where we had anticipated a short holiday before returning to Britain, I found an Officer of the Court waiting for me with a warrant for my arrest! He was carting me off to jail when I spotted Wally Lloyd in the street and he was able to get in touch with our solicitors who, in turn contacted the local magistrate and had me released on bail. I appeared in court the next morning and the case was dismissed, partly because the freight company had been foolish enough to arrest me although they had both of my racing bikes and a lot of my personal effects, more than ample security for the debt that they alleged I owed. Furthermore, our solicitors felt that if I stayed on in

Africa, they could sue the company for heavy damages but as you can appreciate by this time I was only too anxious to get home.

However, our adventures were not at an end because on leaving Jo'burg for our trip to Durban, we had a tremendous send off by a crowd of well wishers who knew nothing of this arrest incident. Then the train on which we were travelling was derailed before we had got very far and we found ourselves back in Jo'burg! We eventually made it to Durban before the news broke in the papers next morning reporting that an English speedway ace had been arrested!'

Just for the record, here are the scorers in that solitary Test Match:

South Africa 17   England 37
    South Africa: Joe Sarkis 5, 'Baby' Scott 4, Alan Reeve 3, Stan Collins 3, Fred Neill 2
    England: Nobby Key 9, John Deeley 9, Ivor Hill 7, Wally Lloyd 5, Bunny Wilcox 4, Charlie Hornby 2,
        Arthur Tims 1

14

The Promoter – the buck stops here

What makes a promoter tick? What makes him risk his all on what is often a gigantic gamble? I asked Hackney and Rye House boss, LEN SILVER what his answers were to these intriguing questions.

'A speedway promoter has to be some kind of a nut; indeed if he were not, then his cash would surely be invested in something far more secure. The weekly bill for staging a British League event amounts to anything from £3000 upwards and it's not difficult to blow the lot when the rain pours down on race-day! Of course, in this high risk business, the rewards **can** be high as well, although it is true to say that most promoters at present earn little more than a good living from the sport they all love. And what does he do to **earn** this living? Well, earn it he certainly does, with long hours of non-stop effort, quite often stretching into the early hours long after more orthodox businessmen have gone to bed.

Although he could not possibly handle all items personally, the promoter is responsible for every aspect of his weekly bill of fare, ranging from the formation and well-being of the team and their equipment, preparation of the track (itself a major task on its own), engagement and supervision of the army of staff, both permanent and temporary, dealing with riders' pay, travelling arrangements and bookings, advertising and public relations and of course, a share in the overall work of organising the sport on a National and International level.

A huge section of each day is devoted to the telephone, whereby he is in constant touch with the gentlemen of the Press, his fellow promoters, the riders and, most of all, the fans who are constantly ringing up to ask about some aspect of the team or next week's meeting. Sometimes it seems to me that I must have been born with a telephone receiver stuck in my left ear!

Usually one day each week is devoted to the compilation of the programme, writing the notes and generally setting it all out ready for the printer. Some promoters, of course, employ specialists to do this for them, but even when they do, they cannot escape the responsibility of seeing that the information to be printed is as factually correct as possible.

The riders today lean very heavily on their promoters to help them with equipment problems and it's a strange promoter who has not had more than one of his riders ring up just hours before a meeting to say 'help' because some engine part has just broken and he hasn't got a replacement. Maybe it was always so, in fact I constantly learn that there is nothing new under the sun and the problems of today's promoter are probably the self same problems of his pre-war counterpart.

My own particular relaxation is to help my permanent track maintenance engineer with his work, relaying, grading and levelling the shale ready for the Friday night meeting at Hackney. The beauty of this is that when the track gets praise from the riders, I can stick out my chest and say 'Thanks fellers, it was nothing!' On the other hand, when it turns out a bit sticky, I can say 'You must moan at Jack, he's in charge of the track!' And the 'Jacks' of speedway take it all in good part, knowing that the promoter does sometimes need some one to pass the blame to, for, just like the President of the United States, on most promoters' desks is a card which reads **The buck stops here.** And there it normally stays!'

VOTE FOR

JOHNNIE BROUGHTON
FRANK CHARLES
LARRY COFFEY
BROADSIDE BURTON
BUSTER BREAKS
CHARLIE BARRETT
ALEC HILL
FRANK HARRISON
NORMAN EVANS

Sure Candidates for the

CLEVELAND PARK
(Speedway Division).

FRIDAY NIGHT next
May 31st, at 7-30 p.m.

___

Labour Exponents of British Skill and Pluck.

Liberal Cinder Shifters.

Conservative Trophy Holders.

Admission (including Tax): Popular Enclosure 1/-.
Both Grand Stands - 2/- each.

Ladies and Children half-price to all parts.

Wokside, Printers, Middlesbro'

One way to advertise! A rather unique way of publicising Middlesbrough (now Teesside) speedway in 1929

15

Track preparation

To know how to prepare a track for racing is of the utmost importance and no one is more aware of this than GEORGE GOWER, ex-West Ham, Leicester, Birmingham rider who looks after the Leicester track and is one of the acknowledged experts on the subject. I asked George about his experiences of some of the tracks with which he had been associated.

"As speedway has developed, so has track preparation, from the fairly primitive to the professional. A good illustration of the former occurred at Barnet when initially I became interested in this side of the sport. The Barnet track was situated in fields alongside the by-pass and I remember one Saturday afternoon George Wilks, Jack Balmer, well known Steward Allen Day, A-CU official Professor Lowe and myself measuring the distance with our feet. To start with, this was just a grass track, but as the grass was torn off it subsequently became a dirt track.

Amongst the attractions at Barnet were the London Corps of Signals, forerunners of today's White Helmets, and I was one of several speedway men to try stunt and trick riding. I toured the circuits on an old Triumph dispatch riders' machine used in the 1914-18 war and, with an army officer on the back, performed my party pieces.

My next track association could not have been closer to home. It was in fact, constructed in fields behind my mother's public house at Sarratt, in Hertfordshire. The Watford Motor Cycle and Auto Club, whose President was Graham Walker of Isle of Man TT racing fame, were seeking a venue to stage Bank Holiday Monday meetings, so we ripped and dug out a dividing hedge to convert two fields of about nine acres into one. I obtained two horses and a plough with which I shaped the circuit and made it into a pukka dirt track — each corner was naturally banked, as the field had a valley through the middle and riders could pick up speed going downhill out of the bends.

In 1950, I was based at St. Austell and this at the time was described as the best riding track in the country. A cinder circuit, here I employed a farming harrow behind a tractor to riddle and separate the dirt, following that with a grader to smooth and level the surface.

During the early days, of course, there was not the same kind of dedication applied to track preparation as there is now. The main idea was to provide a track with as even a top as possible and, bumps or no bumps, the riders just had to go out and ride it. The majority of cinder circuits had bricks for a base, laid roughly level. Then the dirt was thrown on, rolled and watered. Much the same principle still exists with most shale tracks which are brick based, with the shale then rolled and levelled, although some venues have changed to a dressing of granite chippings.

For the last seven seasons I have been responsible for preparing the Leicester track which, although I say it myself, is one of the best in the British League. More modern methods are utilised here, a most important piece of equipment being a knife, the broad blade stretching diagonally across the track and contained in a frame moved by two large wheels at the back and two small ones at the front. The knife, pulled by the tractor, is raised or lowered by two other large wheels, for which I possess chains to lock either in position, and is adjusted by levers. I set the blade according to requirements, for instance so that it cuts more on one side than the other and also freely distributes the shale where I wish. I go round the track for hours, perhaps only altering the setting of the knife by half an inch, cutting high spots off the circuit and transferring the dirt to any low spots, thereby ensuring a super smooth surface. In addition, I maintain the slight banking which enables riders to travel fast into the bends. This gives them something

Track raking at Wimbledon c.1931. On the left, Tiger Stevenson and Vic Huxley pass on their instructions

to bite into and they can take more of a risk, because if the bends are flat or cambered the wrong way, they have nothing to hold them.

One problem at Leicester is that you are never sure what sort of shale is delivered. Sometimes it is a dusty type; on other occasions stony. Both pack down differently which is one reason why a track surface can vary.

Once I have achieved a surface to my satisfaction, I begin tyre packing with a twin-wheel lorry, trying to avoid leaving any imprint. A tanker full of water, sprayed out behind the wheels, is additionally used, wetting and packing the track simultaneously. Both jobs can take many hours to make certain that whatever materials are underneath, they are securely bound together.

The real sweat arrives on the day of the meeting, with watering a critical factor, particularly if in the morning you have no definite idea what the weather is going to be like. If it is sunny or windy, a lot of watering is necessary, but in other circumstances not so much is required. In the last hour or two before racing commences, it is vital to get the water on early so that it penetrates the material and avoids dust later on. Dust is a major bugbear for riders, supporters and nearby residents who perhaps have washing on the line, which is soon smothered. This leads to complaints to local councillors, even Members of Parliament, with demands for the speedway track to be stopped operating. So it can be appreciated when watching Speedway, what a nightmare it has often been for the person preparing the track, for he is always aiming to create conditions which make everybody happy.

At Leicester, I have been known to get into trouble with the promoter and team manager for producing a track that is so good the opposing riders often perform better than the home men and frequently break the track record. This makes the promoter angry! However, I have a simple solution to vindicate myself — I invariably go to the two captains to ask their opinion of the circuit. More often than not, they reply, 'Just grand. It's lovely, George', proving that I have done the job properly and leaving me with nothing to worry about.

So there we are – last season I completed my 50 years in speedway. In that time, I have missed seeing only one World Final, a record of which I am justifiably proud.'

92

16

Referees viewpoint

GORDON LITTLE and GEOFF DALBY are two Referees with a vast amount of practical knowledge of their sport. Knowing them to be outspoken on occasions, I invited them to have their say. First Gordon, who retired in 1977 after many years as one of the top men in his particular field. He thought that he would do a little reminiscing tinged with nostalgia.

"We used to be called Stewards, which was a misnomer, especially at Wembley, where the Stewards are the men who direct the customers to their seats. The word Referee is now used in many sports, but, I think, originally came from the game of soccer, which, in its early days, was controlled by two linesmen, and if they could not agree, there was a third gent stationed near one of the halfway flags, to whom the matter was referred for a final decision, hence the name Referee. I cannot conclude this paragraph without relating an amusing incident concerning this name. When I was in Assisi some 25 years ago, I left the hotel one evening wearing a blazer, upon which I sported the badge of The Football League Referees & Linesmens Association, over the coat of arms was the word Referee. Upon my return, I received VIP treatment, and when I left next morning, the heads of the staff were lined up, with the proprietor at the end. They all bowed and shook hands with me, and the guvnor said 'Nice to have had you sir, it is the first time that we have had the honour of an English judge staying with us'. So much for dictionary translations.

Referees are appointed from a list compiled by the Auto-Cycle Union, and are usually men dedicated to motorcycle sport in general, who have given years of service in riding and organising, for little or no financial reward. Sometimes matches involve a 300-400 miles round trip, with half of this at night, and 12 hours away from home, and in these circumstances he may gross 50p. per hour.

Much controversy has centred around foreign referees – many of you will have seen some in action at Wembley and it is not their fault that they lack experience, as tracks are not so plentiful abroad, and they do not get many appointments to keep them on their toes. I well remember showing one of these gentlemen around Wembley, as I spoke a bit of his language, when Briggo said to me,'... is not the Referee for tonight is he?'I said 'Yes,' and Briggo replied, 'But he has never refereed a speedway meeting in his life, he runs a long-track raceway.' This referee told me that he had his own method of starting. 'Let the gate up first and then put on the green light, then there is no pushing into the tapes.'

Some of our own big events, like Wills' Internationale, are often better spectacles than the World Final, with largely the same riders. Those of us who remember the pre-war Test Matches with Australia, must be aware of a great vacuum in the sport to-day. Then, speedway made headlines in the papers, everyone from little Johnny to Grandma turned up and went wild with excitement, and the terraces were packed. Although crowds have thinned out, the sport is still healthy, with an ever-increasing number of tracks and broadening of horizons.

Having received his first appointment, the Referee goes to the track in good time, to make his pre-racing inspection of everything directly connected, including the track preparation, machines, leathers, crash helmets, safety precautions and first-aid facilities, dressing rooms, and perhaps quiet chat with some of the riders, who, in general, are more affable than they used to be. In the past, referees have been targets for missiles, and one unfortunate finished up in the dressing-room bath.

The Referee then goes to his rostrum, checks the lights, starting gate, etc., and then completes a long questionnaire in the Track Record Book. From then on, he starts the races, applies the regulations appertaining to the riding, and declares the result of each race. Between races he has to complete a programme for the track as well as for himself, and deal with telephone calls, some polite like the changing of riders for the next race, and some not so polite. There must come a time when the referee, like his soccer colleagues, will not be subject to interference from some riders and officials, which although amounting to harassment, does not always constitute a finable offence. The referee is nearly always in the best position to see the racing, is not biassed, and knows more about the regulations than anyone else. Mistakes can be made, but as in all sport, one has to accept the bad breaks as well as the good ones, otherwise the word 'sport' means nothing.

It is not generally known that there are over 300 regulations governing the sport (ten times as many as soccer), but only a fraction of these apply to the actual racing, the others being concerned with tracks, machines, riders, officials, judicial procedure, etc., but it is one thing to know regulations and another to apply them at a second's notice. Whenever anything goes wrong, no matter what decision the referee makes, it will be approved by one section of the crowd and officials, and disapproved by the other. In tape-breaking incidents, very often the referee excludes the wrong offender, if he is a home rider, but the right one if he is a visitor. Crowds have a parochial outlook, by and large. Therefore, the Referee must be strictly impartial at all times, meting out the same treatment to each side, likewise to star or novice. I well remember when Jack Young was at his peak, he was booked in for the second half at Wembley, Heat, and Final if he made it, with guaranteed appearance money. In the Heat, Jack anticipated the start and completely demolished the tapes. I excluded him, and the Wembley Manager, the late Duncan King, immediately telephoned me and said that Sir Arthur Elvin (a member of the SCB) would go mad, as it had cost him a large booking fee, and Jack would not be eligible for the Final. I had to remind him of the words printed in his programme, 'Held under the Regulations of the Speedway Control Board.' Although it was an easy decision to make, it was a very painful one, as Wembley were lavish in their hospitality, and the Referee and his wife were always invited to partake of dinner afterwards, with the Manager and his wife.

Appeals may be made upon any decision made by the Referee, who shall deal with the matter immediately. If the appellant is not satisfied, he may appeal to the SCB. These appeals can only succeed where the Referee has made a mistake in applying the regulations such as allowing a reserve too many rides. There is no appeal against a Referee's decision on incidents occurring during racing. If the Referee says that it occurred, it occurred. Otherwise, there would be endless argument and racing could not continue. Imagine what would happen if a footballer was fouled on the edge of the box, and players and officials started arguing whether or not it was a penalty. Some riders and officials are notorious among Referees for their continual harassment. They should be warned, and fined for a repetition, as continual harassment can intimidate.

Ignorance of the regulations has brought many a rider and official into trouble, and trying to pull a fast one is not unknown. I well remember one famous rider who was dreaming at the starting gate. When it went up, he did not move, but expected me to stop the race, and order a restart. I had no reason to do so, as the other riders made a perfect start. After the race, I saw him walk to the telephone. I had anticipated this, and as soon as he picked up the receiver I said, 'Reg., didn't anyone tell you that you are supposed to go when the gate goes up?' There was no answer to that, and we have been good friends ever since.

Speedway has always had its great showmen, whether it be Promoters like Johnny Hoskins, or riders like Bruce Abernethy, Split Waterman, Oliver Hart, or Howdy Byford, but they seem a bit thinner on the ground these days. Of course, the really greats like Vic Duggan, Jack and Norman Parker, Bill Kitchen, Ronnie Moore, Barry Briggs, and Ivan Mauger, were too good and too safe to be as spectacular as some, especially the leg trailers. My 'all time best' must be Ronnie Moore. I knew him throughout his career, and never once did I have to admonish him, and neither have I seen other Referees do so. Not only did he, at one time or another, win every great event, but he was the greatest captain and team rider I have ever had the pleasure of knowing.

There are not many of the old-time promoters left either. Johnnie H. has always been a great showman. More than ever, speedway is becoming showbiz, and less of a motorcycle sport. Johnnie and I have always had a close understanding, and when one of his riders is penalised, he strides over the arena to the telephone, and makes a mock protest to impress the crowd, who cheer Johnnie, whilst we are exchanging a few friendly salutations, well-coloured with terms in the vernacular.

Another great showman was Charlie Knott, not as spectacular as Johnnie, but always eager to put on a good show. When I used to referee regularly at Southampton, Charlie often put on an extra race. Invariably the riders were Bjorn Knutson, Barry Briggs, Peter Craven, and Ove Fundin, the last three being either members of the Visiting Team, or booked in as a second-half attraction. These races were obviously fixed, as the first three went around for four laps only feet apart, sending the crowd wild with excitement, and I could never understand why the fourth always kept about ten lengths behind the others, until one night the secret was revealed to me by Peter. We often met at a Fish Restaurant on the way home, and I asked him how the race was fixed. He said that they were paid £5 each, irrespective of how they finished, with orders to make it look good. This race remained the talking point among spectators for days, and produced as much excitement as the leg-trailers of yesteryear.

94

Many years ago, a famous referee reported that a Match Race Championship had been fixed, the SCB ordered an investigation, but the whole matter fizzled out through lack of evidence. I was once concerned in a World Championship qualifying round, where, on the last lap of the last race the leader slowed down to let a team-mate win. The erstwhile leader had already qualified, and the extra point also allowed his team-mate to qualify. I imposed a maximum fine of £5 upon the offending rider, and also told him that the incident would be reported to the SCB for further action, as it brought the game into disrepute. After the meeting, the co-promoters were very abusive, in spite of the fact that I had explained to them that, not only did I have to administer the law at that meeting, but the repercussions could affect other riders at the lower end of the qualifying zone. They said that they would have my name removed from the List of Referees. My reply was to fine them £20 each on the spot, and to report them to the SCB for further action.

Some regulations are changed so often that Referees are sometimes bewildered when they have to make a quick decision. The worst one to deal with is that governing the number of rides a reserve may have, and many a Referee and Team Manager have come unstuck on this one.

In my opinion, far too much gamesmanship has crept in, mainly in pre-start tactics, such as leaving the pits late and fiddling around on the starting grid, in order that the other riders may get their plugs woolly or burn out their clutches; pushing into the tapes in order to entice less experienced riders to break them; or rocking to and fro. I often fine them for delaying the start, and issue a warning that a repetition will lead to exclusion, although they may not break the tapes. Many years ago, when Wembley were the opponents at Wimbledon, everything depended on the last race, when Wembley wanted a 4-2 to force a draw. In those days, the starting area was marked out in rectangles called grids, and there was a regulation which said, 'Any rider going out of his grid with either wheel, before the gate is released, shall be excluded, 'One of the Wembley riders did just that. He went right over the tapes, his machine had to be lifted off, but the tapes did not break. I invoked the law, the Wembley reserve rider was not equal to the occasion, and Wimbledon won. Of course, there were the usual protests that the rider had not broken the tapes, and that my decision had ruined the match, but it was the foolhardiness of the excluded rider which did that. At the end of the meeting, I had to leave via the Press Box, and the late Jim Stenner queried my decision. I showed him the regulation, and he said to the rest of the Press Boys, 'There can be no argument about that.'

In conclusion may I offer this advice. To all riders and officials, learn the Regulations thoroughly. To all Promoters, please standardise your programmes, so that the users may have room to write in alternations. To all riders and mechanics, thoroughly clean and maintain your machines and protective clothing. Remember that a well oiled chain has twenty times the strength of a dry and rusty one and do not argue with the referee, no matter how strong your feelings may be. You would not do so with a Judge in a Court of Law and remember that the Law must always be paramount."

Geoff Dalby has his own store of memories and experiences and observations.

"My introduction to the shale game was in 1949 when Leicester reopened after the war. The Hunters, as they were then known, raced in the National League Division 3, and visiting teams at Blackbird Road included Yarmouth, Liverpool, Plymouth, Rayleigh, Tamworth and Hastings, which, sadly, no longer operate for one reason or another. Amongst those wearing the colours of Hunting Pink and Gold were Roy Duke, Cyril Page, Harwood Pike, Vic Pitcher, George Gower, Ted Rawlinson, Ron Wilson, Ted Moore, Syd Van de Vyver, Jackie Gates, Johnny Carpenter and Pedlar Palmer. At that time, an A-C.U. Steward was the man in charge ably supported by an A-C.U. Judge/Timekeeper and I never thought then, as I paid my 9d entrance money, (programmes 6d.) that 20 years later I would be an A-C.U. official. After a few meetings, I was really hooked on these shale sliders and began to get more involved with programme marking and learning the regulations.

Speedway has changed immensely since the formation of the British League and regulations have also come in for some alterations. The introduction of tactical substitutes, silencer regulations and more rigid safety regulations have all been changes for the better. Safety is my number one priority at any meeting and the notices displayed at all tracks remind us that speedway racing is dangerous.

Testimonial meetings for riders with 10 years or more service to one track has been a welcome introduction and long serving riders to benefit have included Ray Wilson, Norman Storer, Nigel Boocock, Bob Paulson, Terry Betts, Mike Keen and Soren Sjosten. It was my pleasure to officiate at the bonanza meetings of both Terry Betts and Nigel Boocock and what enjoyable, memorable occasions they were. These riders deserved all the benefit they received and I trust that many more of the speed and thrill merchants will gain some reward in the future.

After many years as a paying spectator, I first ventured into administration of the sport in 1963, when Long Eaton re-opened after Leicester had closed, following a poor season in the old Provincial League. Arriving at Station Road early one Tuesday, I was pressed into action on security by Mrs. Joan Fearman. That was the start and in the following years I was employed as co-ordinator between the pits and the

A rolling start at Belle Vue in 1932. Riders are Eric Langton, Vic Huxley, Frank Charles, and Claude Rye (N.J. McAinsh)

referee's rostrum. Then prior to my appointment as Trainee Referee, I was Clerk of the Course at the Derbyshire track. I accepted the challenge as a Trainee Referee because I felt I could do the job and my experience of speedway pit duties together with my motorcycling club grass track activities helped a lot.

After a season and half of training, I officiated for the first time without supervision on 2nd June 1969 at Earle Street, Crewe. The visitors were Teesside and I remember they included Bruce Forrester, a newcomer then, a reserve who was later to reach the heights. Since this first meeting as the 'man in charge' I have had my moments of glory and I have also had my share of controversy too.

On the glory side, I enjoyed refereeing the British Final in 1973 and many other, thrilling individual, league, cup and international test matches. On the reverse side, I recall some strong criticism when I refused to allow the Newport v Sheffield British League match to start on 22nd August 1975, because the red stop lights were completely out of action at Somerton Park. A Speedway Control Board inquiry into the matter confirmed that my decision was correct and in 1976, regulations were amended to incorporate an emergency procedure.

Controversy often arises after a race is stopped on the last lap in the interests of safety. If a rider has fallen on the third lap and it is considered dangerous for the race to continue, very often the other riders in the race are on the last lap when the race is stopped. Regulation 214 states quite clearly that unless the leading rider has taken the chequered flag, the race must be re-run. The trouble starts because the team (or rider) that was nicely placed at the time of the stoppage want the race to stand according to the position at that time. On the other hand, quite naturally, riders not so well placed are quite happy to have another chance to improve their respective positions.

In spite of any controversy, riders, officials and referees usually have a good relationship and even after disputes, which are often over-dramatised in the press, things are soon forgotten and the next meeting is another day.

Builder of the starting gate – Harry Shepherd

Harry's partner at Crystal Palace for many years, England International Joe Francis, later associated with Brands Hatch racing circuit

The man who invented the starting gate, one of the greatest showmen/promoters of all time, Fred Mockford, seen talking to ex-England and Odsal star Ron Clarke

When the season ends, the winter months give promoters, riders and officials time to discuss the past season's problems and to plan for the new season. The Association of Speedway Referees have their own meetings and during the past few years have also had joint get-togethers with the BSPA, SCB, A-CU and SRA. As Chairman of the ASR in 1976, my Committee and I met the Chairman and Committee of the SRA and several proposals made at this meeting and accepted by the authorities include the one specifying that an ambulance shall be in attendance at all speedway race meetings.

Winter activities organised by speedway supporters clubs over the last few years have brought forth many invitations and I have attended, and contributed to, many enjoyable evenings which have included a talk-in, speedway quiz, forum, dinner/dances, film shows, speedway darts and bring and buy sales. Clubs visited include Peterborough SC, Leicester SC, Nuneaton SC, South Leicestershire SC, Shale-Searchers SC, where the club officers have always been very hospitable. It is always a pleasure to attend these functions and clubs need not be afraid to invite a Referee to participate."

17

Reminiscences of a Senior A-C.U. referee

A Referee's job can be very exacting and on occasions extremely controversial and it is always interesting to get his views on Speedway topics. No one has had greater all round experience in the game than ARTHUR HUMPHREY, the Senior A-C.U. Referee and I asked him to talk about his 30 years in charge.

'When I start to recall my early years in speedway, I find that memories come flooding back just as much about tracks, personalities, crowds and promoters as about actual racing. Of those tracks about which I have fond or not-so-fond memories are some no longer operating – High Beech, Hastings, Rayleigh, Walthamstow, Wembley and many others.

Hastings, situated in a smart part of the seaside town where, during the efforts of local factions to get the track closed, it was alleged that small children could be seen on race nights begging for money from the riders when in fact, they were asking for autographs! Handsome Buddy Fuller, the popular South African, who rode for them suffered terrible injuries to the face in a crash, necessitating the wearing of a plastic brace in, and projecting from, his mouth to support his jaw for months afterwards.'

Rayleigh, run in the 1950's by Arthur and 'Tippy' Atkinson, with Ron Howes and Charlie Mugford (now in Australia) in the team had, on the track by the start, a small glass building, just big enough for two people at the most. On race nights around the base of this little glass house were packed potted flowers, with their earth-filled pots towards the inside and the blooms facing outwards, giving the illusion of a bank of blossom. During a meeting when sidecar racing was in progress, racing clockwise as they do, one combination got out of control and, shedding its passenger, crashed at high speed into the little building. The earth in the pots had the effect of forming a bank of soil which lifted machine and sidecar into the air. The outfit smashed the whole timber frame and glass into smithereens, ripped out the electricity cables and put the stadium in darkness. Mrs. Atkinson who was inside with the starting-line marshal, Jack Agambar, ducked down and the careering machine passed safely over her prostrate body, but Jack Agambar, who had remained upright and was endeavouring to get out, took glass and machine in his face. He had only one sighted eye and when I saw him with his face just a mass of blood looking like a red sponge I had fears for his sight. His wife and son, both of whom worked in the stadium, doubtless felt the same way. However, Jack was a tough baby and not only recovered but also returned to his job on the line, albeit after a long recovery.

Walthamstow, with extrovert Bruce Abernethy always up to some prank or another,was the track which numbered Donald Peers, the current heart throb, and a very youthful Petula Clark in its fan club. Aldershot, situated at Tongham near the garrison town, was where the local fire engine was pressed into service for watering the track during one of my visits.

Harringay was where the gentlemanly Aub Lawson used to ride, together with Ron How and Jack Biggs, and where Tom Stenner and son Jim with George Kay, diminutive but efficient used to run things. Celebrities of the time were always to be seen at Harringay, including McDonald Hobley, Kenneth Horne and Dicky Murdoch and, on one occasion, the whole Australian Test Team.

When Billy Graham, the evangelist, was in Britain, he used the nearby Harringay Arena for his services. On speedway nights the stadium was almost completely empty – so much so that Tom Stenner said he would let the public in to the speedway free, to get a gate. This was not allowed, however, and for the rest of Billy Graham's stay Harringay ran with almost no spectators.

At Elstree, a local farmer prepared a track by pouring oil onto a field for the first meeting on Sunday 10th August 1947. Most of the top riders rode, the line up including Bill Kitchen, Cyril Brine, Tiger Hart,

Bob Wells, Freddie Williams and Roy Craighead. The only covered accommodation was a canvas marquee which served as a dressing room, changing room and everything else. The track did not last long and I refereed all the meetings there but while it was operating it attracted big crowds and had sideshows such as beauty contests and knobbly knees competitions during the intervals.

New Cross, in the New Kent Road area, was where I fined a rider or two for not making a bona-fide attempt to win their races after which, in the interval, the ageless Johnnie Hoskins put over the PA: 'If the gentleman who said that my riders were not trying would like to come down here, I will take great pleasure in punching him on the nose!' I should add that I am still as friendly with Johnnie now and hold him in just as high regard as I did then.

At Rye House, the old track was in a different place from that used now. It had a safety fence of sheets of corrugated steel that was most unpleasant to collide with. To overcome any objections to Sunday racing by the Lord's Day Observance Society, the local vicar was asked to give a short sermon in the interval, apparently thoroughly enjoying the racing before and after his contribution. Rye House was where the Referee's box was then on the infield, next to the start line. This made it necessary to turn round and round each lap as the race progressed. Consider the ridiculous situation arising out of this set-up when, if the four riders were dicing in two pairs half a lap apart, the poor Referee was expected to watch all four when he had one pair in his sight, as it were, while the other two were going past the back of his head.

Yarmouth was another track where the Referee's box was on the infield and where I saw a young Australian novice go progressively faster in an effort to catch up with the others. Finally he hit the last-bend fence, projected himself onto the starting area (then concrete) and literally wore his helmet and skull away as he slid along. At the inquest, the Chief Constable and most of the jury turned out to be Yarmouth fans.

Then there was Wembley. Fabulous marvellous Wembley – the track with everything. This was the track where the Promoter A.J., later to become Sir Arthur Elvin, would not have a vocal record player over the PA and where the organisation was so strict that even the rakes had to be placed crosswise like swords in a sword dance when not being used. The price of admission included a dance in the restaurant after the meeting and a variety turn during the interval.

At one of these interval attractions there was a gentleman who called himself Dare Devil Peggy or Peg Leg Peggy, who had only one leg, the other having been removed at the thigh. He used to climb slowly and laboriously, hopping on his one leg, rung by rung up a slender ladder on a 60 feet high lattice steel tower, specially erected in the centre of the green. From there, having made the climb, he would project himself into space and dive into a container shaped like a saucepan that was about 8 feet in diameter and 6 feet deep. It was full of water and covered with blazing petrol.

Oh, and just to make things a little more interesting, before taking off he would be drenched in an inflammable liquid and set fire to himself. This was a marvellous act which used to fascinate and horrify me, and I still can't see how he did not smash himself to pieces on the bottom of his outsized pot. Rumours were current at the time that Peg Leg was developing his act by gradually reducing the amount of water until finally he would dive into a damp rag. But they were discounted as being untrue.

At Wembley the track lighting was made up of lamps of differing colours which combined to give a dazzling white light ideal for racing. The Referee's box, situated high above the stands, gave a perfect view of every nudge of the elbow and thrust of the feet of the riders at every point on the circuit. It was said that some correspondents could report on a match without leaving the bar. In the late 1940's, it was necessary to be at the stadium around 4.30 pm to be sure of a seat at 7.45 p.m.

In addition to many other International events I was selected to be Referee for the World Championship Finals of 1954, 1963 and 1967. It is the highest honour for a Referee to be chosen for a world final, and a word of explanation as to how he qualifies for such selection will not be amiss. Only an FIM-registered Referee can officiate at an event held under an FIM permit. (FIM is short for Federation Internationale Motorcycliste, the controlling body for all worldwide competitive motorcycle sport, based in Geneva). All countries have a body which operates the FIM sporting code, the British one being our own Auto-Cycle Union, and the West German the Oberste Motorradsport Kommission, to name but two. To be elevated to FIM status, a Referee must be extremely highly thought of by the A-CU to be nominated and, even then, it does not follow that he will be given international meetings, and certainly not world-championship appointments. I was fortunate enough to be elevated to International rank some twentyfive years ago and, besides the three world-championship finals mentioned above, have refereed similar events in Sweden and West Germany.

The FIM Sporting Code is a set of regulations covering all motor cycle events and, while the speedway regulations contained therein are largely similar to the British regulations, some differ in small detail. For example, the elastic on the tapes must be no longer than 100 mm under the FIM Code but there is no limit written into the British regs; also a reserve replaces a rider excluded for tape-breaking in an individual event under FIM rules, but not in a team or pairs event, whereas in British speedway the reserve is permitted in both.

To referee a world-class event is a vastly different experience from officiating at ordinary speedway meetings. To begin with, at every World-Championship fixture there is an FIM steward who is senior to the Referee and whose job it is to see that the organisation is up to standard and to be the adviser in any dispute that cannot be settled by the Referee. He reports back to the FIM, giving details of attendance, starts, fuel sampling and noise. He also reports on the performance of the Referee. Although these FIM stewards have wide powers, in practice they do not interfere with the Referee and are kind and helpful. Those I have worked with have come from Sweden, Germany, Holland, Italy and the United States of America.

Having been appointed to a World-Championship meeting, the Referee is expected to attend the practice, usually held a day or two days before the actual meeting. For practice purposes, riders are separated into groups from countries or regions, thus Scandinavia, Australia, USSR and so on, all being allocated so much time on the track and given so many starts. This gives some semblance of racing conditions and prevents too many riders being on the track at the same time.

Another requirement introduced in recent years is the measuring of noise. No machine may be noisier than 110 decibels under the prescribed test (this to be even lower in 1979). A noteworthy difference between FIM and British rules in this connection is that whereby the exhaust system on a machine used in Great Britain must have an approved pattern silencer or muffler, in an FIM event a straight-through pipe is allowed provided its emission is not higher than the maximum permitted decibel reading. All machines have to be examined to see that they conform to the construction regulations and, after a world final, those occupying the first three places have their engines measured to ensure that they are within a cubic capacity of 500. These measuring jobs, both for noise and capacity, are carried out in England by Ernie Woods, a great character who has been around the speedway scene for a long time.

My first World-Championship final was in 1954 and those who took part make interesting recollections, not only on account of names unknown to many of today's fans, but because Barry Briggs was a contestant, who is still riding 23 years later. The big names were Jack Young, already twice a winner (in 1951 and 1952) and widely tipped by the media to win his third crown, Peter Craven, at nineteen one of the youngest competitors, Eddie Rigg, Brian Crutcher, Ove Fundin, at that time quite unable to speak English and having to rely on Olle Nygren to interpret for him, Aub Lawson, Geoff Mardon, Ronnie Moore, who had started riding at fifteen and who rode this final with a special knee support because of an injury which had seemed likely to prevent him from taking part, Arthur Forrest, Jack Biggs, Fred Brand, Barry Briggs, making his first appearance in a World Final, Tommy Price, then aged 43 and winner of the 1949 World Title, Split Waterman, runner-up to Jack Young in 1951 and in 1953 to Freddie Williams, and Captain of Harringay, Olle Nygren, Trevor Redmond and the two reserves, Alan Hunt and Freddie Williams.

Ronnie Moore won the title, damaged knee notwithstanding, and Crutcher and Nygren both finished with thirteen points after twenty heats.

The 1954 final was a fairly peaceful affair but my second, in 1963, was anything but. Only Barry Briggs, Ove Fundin and Peter Craven of those in the 1954 line-up were riding again, the others being Nigel Boocock, Jim Lightfoot, Sverre Harrfeldt, Dick Fisher, Peo Soderman whom I was glad to meet last year in Sweden (he is now no longer riding but doing pit marshal in Norkopping, where I refereed the Nordic final), Peter Moore, Bjorn Knutsson, Ron How, Boris Samorodov, Gote Nordin, P. Svensson, A. Carlsson and Leo McAuliffe. The reserves were Teo Teodorowicz, to die tragically some time later after lying unconscious for six months following a simple-looking fall at West Ham, and Ron Mountford, replacement for the absent A. Kasper.

Heats one and two were smooth enough, but in Heat three Fundin reared at the gate but still led Briggs, How and the Russian, Boris Samorodov, who, giving it all the throttle he had, belted into Ron How and put him down like a shot rabbit. I excluded him and nearly started an International incident. His Manager, Vasily Krivoskeem, went berserk in the pits. He protested that he would withdraw Samorodov if I did not allow him in the rerun. Samorodov, in the meantime, would not leave the track and when the other three riders came out for the re-run he joined them on the way to the start while the crowd were yelling 'off, off'.

I did not give a damn for all this and Boris stayed excluded. Stangely enough, there was no bad blood between him and me as a result of this little fracas and, in the years following, we became quite friendly. Ove Fundin won the re-run and then went on to take the title for his fourth time, but if Samorodov had not been excluded as described, he would almost certainly have won the Championship. He had dropped only one point in his four rides and I feel he would have beaten Fundin in any run-off as he had already beaten Craven and Knutsson, both of whom were tipped as favourites. Peter Craven blew his chances with a couple of falls, one earning him an exclusion.

Coincidentally, my third World Final, in 1967, was again won by Fundin. It gave him his fifth title, a record which has still not been broken although the 1977 champion, Ivan Mauger, has equalled it. The line-up included Mauger, who was third, and the finishing order was, Fundin, B. Jansson, I. Mauger, I. Plechanov the Russian, B. Briggs, Eric Boocock, A. Michanek, Ray Wilson, B. Persson, A. Pogorzelski, A. Woryna, Rick France, Colin Pratt (who is still on the speedway scene managing Rye House), J. Treskowski, A. Wyglenda and J. Dinse of East Germany. Worthy of mention is that in this final, JAP engines were used by only three competitors, Fundin, Mauger and Pratt. Although two of them were in the first three, it was the shape of things to come. Jansson, the Swede, was mounted on an ESO fitted with a Wal Phillips injector, and was beaten twice only, both times by Fundin, the second time in the run-off for first place.

In Heat eighteen, surely the heat in any world final calculated to be full of incident, Fundin made a good start from Mauger, who tried to match him round the bend, but Persson came underneath and put him down. I excluded Persson but this did nothing to please the Swedes in the pits – or the rider himself, who had been involved earlier in a race with Briggs which had resulted in Briggs' falling. Briggs had been adjudged blameless and allowed to take part in the rerun, and Persson considered that he should also be allowed to ride, losing sight of the fact that, in this case, he was the putterdowner and not the put down. Telephones were buzzing from pits to Referee and Persson would not leave the line in spite of a hostile crowd. The other three riders showed reluctance to come to the start and it was not until I had threatened to exclude all three that they appeared, and Persson went back to the pits.

Fundin went on to win his fifth crown, but it took a run-off with compatriot Bengt Jansson to settle the issue. Barry Briggs, who had been hoping that it would be he who would get the fifth title, had an off night, and there was speculation as to whether he would carry on, but Barry shrugged his shoulders philosophically and said 'I suppose it is just one of those things. There's always next year'

Yet another very controversial meeting I refereed at Wembley was the final of the **Daily Mirror** International Speedway Tournament between England and Sweden in 1973. The supplementary regulations for this event decreed that, in the event of a tie on points, there would be a two-man run-off with one rider from each team nominated. Yes, you've guessed it! Both teams had 39 points after thirteen heats, and a run-off was necessary.

A youthful and up-and-coming Peter Collins was chosen for England, and Anders Michanek for Sweden. Collins broke first and led Michanek to the pits bend on the second lap when the Swede rode underneath Collins and down he went. I immediately excluded Michanek under Speedway Regulation 210 (foul or dangerous riding) and awarded the match to England. Pandemonium broke out in the pits, with the Swedes alleging that Michanek should not be put out as he did not touch Collins but there was no doubt in my mind that he had, and the television showing of the incident confirmed it. A word of explanation about the way in which regulations apply to situations like this will not be amiss here. Firstly, the regulation says clearly that the fouled rider does not have actually to be touched by the offender and it also says that there can be no protest or appeal against a Referee's decision as to foul riding. Secondly, such races with only two riders become subject to match-race regulations where the race is not stopped if one rider falls although the offending rider is excluded by the appropriate exclusion light. Obviously there would be no point in stopping the race and ordering a re-run with only one rider eligible to take part. However, the best way of seeing the justice of Michanek's exclusion in this case or, indeed, any rider in a similar case, is to pose the question: 'If Michanek had not been there would Collins have fallen.' Of course he would not have, so it must have been a result of Michanek's action that he came down, and the Swede was rightly excluded for it.

Wimbledon, still running of course, is the scene of many memories and, with the River Wandle close by, a track which used to flood in extreme weather. An apocryphal story which went the rounds and, indeed, still persists, is that on one very wet night when the track was literally under water, Ronnie Greene rowed me round in a boat and when we had finished a complete circuit but not before, I pronounced the track 'unfit for racing'. Wimbledon was where the fabulous Jack Young used to ride as if on rails, never putting a foot or wheel wrong, but he had one bad night and finally left the stadium without permission in high dudgeon, after I had excluded him. He was reported to the Speedway Control Board and, at the disciplinary hearing, was fined £100, a great deal of money in those days.

Billy Ternent and Robin Richmond, respectively a band leader and an organist of the day, never missed a meeting at Wimbledon. Robin even had his instrument brought to the track and set up on the infield to play during the interval but, unfortunately, it rained heavily on both organ and soloist, to the detriment of both and the abandonment of the idea. Ronnie Greene, the promoter, was never short of original ideas and, for a time, used to allow selected spectators on the inside of the track at the bends as this is a spot from where the racing looks most exciting.

In July 1953 I refereed a best-pairs meeting at Wimbledon. It was notable for the fact that Mr. Greene was hit on the head, fair and square, by a large apple thrown, some said, by a member of the Press, while he struggled to part riders fighting in the pits. Events started with the sixth heat. At the first attempt to run it Arthur Payne came a cropper on the first bend and the race was stopped with Payne stretchered off and taking no further part in the meeting. Cyril Brine replaced him in the re-run and then followed what must be one of the most spectacular crashes ever. Jeff Lloyd, Alan Hunt and Brine went down like nine pins. Brine was thrown fully 20 yards along the track and was taken to hospital with a bad head wound. Hunt and Lloyd managed to walk back to the pits, and then Hunt blacked out. After the re-run an argument developed in the pits and it was while he was endeavouring to separate the fighting riders that Ronnie Greene received his gift of fruit. During this little unprogrammed show and while in the thick of it, Ronnie Greene accidentally charged Split Waterman to the ground and poor Split had to go to hospital and return the next day for an X-ray. By this time the crowd were screaming and when, after the final race, Mr. Greene told them that the Wembley brothers, Eric and Freddie Williams, had won the Astorias Trophy, they did not see it that way at all. Film star Gene Anderson, who was there to present the prizes, stood rooted to the spot, petrified by the uproar, while all attempts to speak over the PA were drowned by catcalls. The Wembley pair sportingly offered to re-run the final race and in it confirmed their earlier placings, so putting the issue beyond doubt. I left the track at around midnight with Len Went, then Editor of **Speedway News** who wrote in the next issue that I had said 'Don't want too many nights like that'. He said he agreed with me but was glad I had been officiating.

Strangely enough, referees' boxes have many memories of the early days for me. They differ widely in siting and accommodation, some being on top of the grandstand, others situated among, and in close proximity to, the crowd. As for accommodation, where one or two have the Referee on his own, others have Announcer, Timekeeper and even the Press in with him, a most unsatisfactory arrangement.

The box at Oxford is at the top of a stairway leading from the stand, and access is easy from the public enclosure. Once, when I had excluded a very well-known first-division rider, the door of the box burst open and his wife, an attractive lady smartly dressed and with a nice blonde hair-do, screamed at me 'What do you mean by excluding my husband and depriving him of his livelihood' etc. I told her as politely as I could that the same applied to all riders and that had it not been her husband I would have done just the same. 'Yes' she replied ' that's because you're a ....', using a four letter word I had never heard a lady use before, or since, for that matter.

At Rayleigh, the referee's box was on the top of the building which houses the bar and cafe. Back in the fifties, I had made several decisions during a league match there which displeased the visiting supporters. A group of them congregated below and in front, looking up at me obviously with feelings as hot as a two-dollar pistol, muttering imprecations and making menacing gestures the while. As it was only part-way through the match, I was reassured that they would soon forget and disappear or disperse into the crowd, but by a heat or two from the end of racing they were still there.

I considered this to be a singularly apt time for discretion to be the better part of valour as I needed a confrontation with disgruntled fans then about as much as a tom cat needs a marriage licence. So I took evasive action by climbing over the roof of the cafe to the back, where it was dark and the homegoing crowds were making their way out, I shinned down a handy pipe and joining them with my collar up around my ears, shoulders hunched, and hands deep in my pockets in an endeavour to make myself as unnoticeable as possible.

During the interval there had been a display of ponies both riding and jumping. The animals were still there to be seen and admired, and a small girl who was being dragged unwillingly along by her mother right next to me complained, 'I want to stay and see the horses!' to which mum replied 'Do you, all I want to see is that bloody Referee' I gathered up my tent like an Arab and stole silently into the night.

On another occasion I went into the gent's toilet just before the start of a meeting and saw a morose gentleman with his forehead pressed against the tiles and a programme which he was studying in deep gloom. On realising I was there he gave me a dig in the ribs and a sidelong glance, and uttered in a despairing tone, 'See this' 'No, what' I asked, to which he rejoined 'This' he said, stubbing his finger on the list of officials. 'Humphrey's on tonight, that's buggered it'. He then returned to close study of the programme, having convinced at least the company assembled that all hope of success for the home team had disappeared with the handicap of being controlled by such a Referee. I adjusted my dress before leaving, as exhorted by the notices on the walls, and crept out without reply, but with a more than usually deflated ego.

Speedway racing on the Continent is different from that in England in that it is usually organised at club level and is not a commercial undertaking. The tracks have fewer meetings; in fact one in West Germany, north of Hamburg, where I have officiated, has only three a year. None of the track staff gets paid and the rakers, pushers-off, clerk of the course etc. all give their services free, for the love of the sport. Perhaps because of the small number of meetings the gates are large and besides being charged 15 marks (about £3.75) entrance fee, the public are admitted for the practice, for which a charge of 5 marks (£1.25) is made. At the meeting I did in 1977, the Continental semi-final of the World

103

Championship, some 5,000 watched the practice, and 18,000 the semi-final. Additionally, it is usual for the brewers to pay so much for each spectator who attends, providing their beer is sold exclusively! Organisation and preparation is extremely good and, at this track, the Referee's box had double glazed windows, electronic timing, was brick built and everything was clinically clean. The track equipment included four tractors, three ambulances, a rubber tyred mechanical roller and, at the pits entrance facing inwards, were a green and a red light controlled from the referee's box, which the Referee would use by switching on the red one if he was not ready for the riders or the green one if he wanted them to hurry up.

In Sweden, a beautiful country with wide, straight roads and a population smaller than that of London, the Referee and the FIM steward are treated with great kindness and respect, and are given the full VIP treatment. When I did a Nordic final at a track in the north of the country, at my inspection on the day before the meeting I found a soft patch on the bend likely to present a hazard, and several other small things which did not conform to the FIM Code. On having these pointed out to them the organisers not only worked into the night putting them right, including taking up, relaying and consolidating the track at the soft area together with rectifying the other faults, they even had the signs on the controls in the referee's box repainted in English. All this was done before morning. Referees' decisions are accepted on the Continent without argument, and there is none of the dissent from riders who sit on the gate without 'digging the garden' as is so prevalent over here.

There was a restaurant some half mile from the track. It was used by the organisers of the speedway and the facility was extended to me to eat there at no expense to myself. This non-payment arrangement was done in the following way. Before leaving the track the back of one's hand was marked by a rubber stamp with some Swedish words on it which I did not understand. The procedure then was that I and others so stamped selected and enjoyed the marvellous food on offer and, when it was time to settle, instead of paying we just presented our clenched fists to the waitress.

Another thing which struck me as a good idea was a large area of about a square mile near to this restaurant, which is used by young teenage girls and boys to let off their energy on motor cycles or in cars. There is also a workshop where they can do repairs and mods beside knocking out dents gathered on the track.

Looking back on more than 30 years of refereeing a thing that strikes me is the number of promoters whom I controlled years ago when they were riders. Len Silver, Pete Lansdale and Wally Mawdsley, the latter for whom I bought a drink at Rayleigh before his first-ever ride, while telling him not to be nervous. They rode for Exeter, while Reg Fearman rode for West Ham at the time when Eric Chitty and Malcolm Craven were in the Custom House line-up; Danny Dunton, once of Harringay, Bobby Dugard, Eastbourne and Wimbledon. All have watched the green light, waiting for me to switch it on and all have been put out at one time or another. None, I am happy to say, bear any ill-feeling and I am still welcome at their tracks now they are the bosses. For my own part, the progress I have made from the day so many years ago when I took my first meeting in great trepidation is worthwhile and not inconsiderable. I am now the Senior Referee in British speedway, have the widest experience and have worked more meetings, both ordinary and international, than any Referee in the world.'

18

The Machine Examiner

Ask members of the speedway public to define the duties of a Machine Examiner and I guarantee that ninety per cent would be hard put to supply an adequate answer. I therefore asked BILL MATHIESON, who acts in this capacity at Crayford and Rye House, to tell us something about his work in the pits.

'Who would imagine danger in being a Machine Examiner. I hold this post at two speedway tracks and not only assure you it can be dangerous, I have the scars to prove it! Hold on a minute – that doesn't mean I'll do a strip on request!!

I'm not sure whether the danger is greater from some defective part on a bike, or from the anger of the rider when I point it out to him. That's not really true – even when one of the lads apologises for turning the rear wheel just when your finger is testing the chain for slack, you can see the friendly twinkle in his eye. At least I think that's what it is! It does help having known so many of the riders for so long and being considered a friend. Not so good for the rider who being known to have 'questionable' equipment, is found to have put his name tag upon someone else's immaculate machine! "You can't be the examiner, you know us too well" is the cry.

Most of my colleagues must feel the same as I about having to report offences concerning machines or equipment. It is very necessary for this function to be a part of speedway, but we feel badly should we have to point out any contravening of the rules. I'm sure we all carry a reel of sticky tape and a pen to provide a name tag for a lad who has forgotten his. We find it awkward to help the fellow who, in the days when exhaust pipes had to have slots cut in them, painted black slots on the chrome pipe or in the later use of silencers, where the silencer is slid over the exhaust pipe, thus hiding the fact that it is still a straight through! It is a laugh a minute really and these tricks usually mean a scurrying round to obtain the correct parts before start time.

Perhaps it would be a good idea for machine examiners to be trained ballet dancers, and even dress in tights like Nureyev for their duties. After all, if you could see them leaping and swaying about to avoid being run down by machines on a pre-meeting warm-up, I'm sure you would agree!

Being employed by a leading Speedway parts supplier doesn't help in my efforts to avoid the leg pulling that goes on in the pits. As soon as I say "You need a new one" up goes the scream "Here he goes again on a sales drive". It's not even a little bit true, you know, my bonus has nothing to do with it! More so, if I were really to do it my way I'd own a gents' outfitters and insist on all riders appearing in dinner jackets and bow ties. A bouquet to Stan Stevens is due here. He took me literally once and turned out ready to ride in his leathers plus a very smart tie. See – someone listens to me !!

Many folk would give anything to be in the pits at a speedway meeting and as you can see there is a lot of fun to be had. There is however, the sobering thought that if I do not carry out my duties as laid down in regulations for the safety of the riders, then I will be at fault if a lad is hurt, however slightly, through my negligence. As the machine examiner the responsibilities cover helmets, clothing etc. in addition to the bike and through the jokes and leg-pulling must always be the maximum attention to detail.

I am very happy to do a job which is at least ninety per cent for the safety of riders, while at the same time constantly renewing acquaintance with lads from all over the world. Finally, I hope that the riders will always accept my judgement as a contribution to their own safety and not allow it to develop into an argument which could harm our continued friendship'.

19

The Track Announcer

I felt that this book would not be complete without the memoirs of an Announcer and so I managed to twist the arm of popular TED SEAR, who fulfils this role each week at Hackney and here he reveals a few of the hazards that confront the man at the mike.

'I suppose the beginning of Ted Sear – announcer – was really at Rye House. One cold and wintry night in January 1963, yours truly was heard for the first time over a PA system. "The greyhounds are now approaching the starting traps", I stammered nervously. As the meeting continued, my confidence gradually built up and at the end of that cold evening I was told "You'll do". Following that frightening first time before the mike, I joined the Speedway staff at Rye House.

Hackney, of course, opened for speedway in 1963; I was already on the staff there but was only really involved in the greyhound racing. Once again on a very cold and wintry night, I (and many other Speedway enthusiasts this time) made the acquantance of Mike Parker at the Wick Stadium. Promoter M.P. told us of his plans for Speedway at Hackney and called for volunteers for various track duties. "Who wants to be our record player?" said Mike. I volunteered and there must be something in cold nights because I was lucky again and got that job too!

My father first introduced me to speedway at Walthamstow in 1950 and from then on I had followed the Sport avidly. Cycle speedway also featured prominently in my teens and I am still very interested in this sport, which has produced so many of the present day speedway riders. However, I digress; after a few months 'on the turntable' at Hackney, my big moment came when the late Peter Arnold – Hackney's then regular announcer – telephoned to say that he would be unable to get back from the Isle of Man TT Races in time for the Friday meeting and I was asked to stand in. Sadly, it was as a result of Peter's fatal car crash that I was requested to announce in his place at a Wembley World Final. It had always been Peter's ambition to announce at Wembley and it was a tragedy that he should have been prevented from achieving it in 1969. The Empire Stadium on World Final night has of course, a unique atmosphere, but although it turned out to be a nerve racking experience, it was a privilege to be an integral part of the occasion.

'An Announcer's task is to provide the public with information – I always abide by a rule to make personal comments only when complimentary. Accurate pronunciation is one part of the job, which I am particularly keen to achieve. The Embassy of the country concerned is always very helpful and provides the phonetic pronunciation for the different names. You would be surprised how easy difficult Polish names are to pronounce, **after** you have had the benefit of phonetics from the Embassy. I am sure, and in fact know, that all the Continental riders appreciate having their names correctly announced.

'Announcing can at times be quite a lonely occupation, particularly if you are isolated high in the roof of the stadium. Your only contact is the telephone, which sometimes, unfortunately, is not always reliable. On those occasions, I have been forced to engage the services of a "runner", who somehow or other manages to dash through the crowd at breakneck speed from the pits to the box to tell me of a last minute change. The announcement generally is greeted with a groan from the supporters, because the announced change merely reverses an earlier alteration! Programme alterations, particularly last minute ones are irritating, I know, but it isn't always the announcer's fault – mistakes there can be and at the time of error, you know that you are not really alone!'

So don't be too hard on Ted who hopes to be talking to you sometime during the season.

20

Speedway tapes; a new entertainment

Speedway tapes seem to be in vogue these days, so I asked WALLY LOAK, originator of this form of entertainment how it started.

'It all began in 1955 when I knocked on the Speedway Office door at the Blackbird Road Stadium, the home of the old Leicester Hunters. Squib Burton (England star of the 'thirties) was the manager and he agreed to my request for a small supply of electricity to enable me to make my first speedway recording the following week, when Southampton were the visitors. Then in 1959, I purchased my first portable recorder – a Stuzzi two speed open reel machine which gave me much more scope.

I made my first trip abroad in 1964 (to Sweden) for the World Final. I shall never forget it, rain, rain, rain from 1.30 pm onwards for six hours. No way, I thought, can this meeting go on but with my entrance ticket already in my pocket, I dejectedly splashed my way through ever increasing puddles to the Ullevi Stadium. What a night! 600 bags of sawdust enabled the meeting to be raced and with Barry Briggs winning the Championship, it was all worthwhile. I shall never forget the bunch of English sailors throwing their white hats into the air as Barry went round on his lap of honour.

Later on, back home in sunny England I wondered whether speedway fans who hadn't been able to travel to Sweden might like the opportunity of listening to the excitement of a recording in the comfort of their homes. Needless to say the idea was successful and I regained the money paid out on my air fare. The seed was sown and ever since, I have paid my way in my complex speedway-cum-sports tapes hobby and in fact, I have been able to send donations to the Speedway Riders' Benevolent Fund'.

A Royal occasion. HRH The Duke of Edinburgh presents Vic Duggan with the Riders Championship Cup in 1948. In the background are Alex Statham and Ron Johnson (Lewis W. Gale)

108

Team records

BARROW

British League. Div. 2. 1972 (9th) 1973 (10th) 1974 (12th)
National League. 1978 (20th)

Leading Riders: 1972 – Bob Coles and Mike Sampson
                          1973 – Tom Owen and Mike Sampson
                          1974 – Tom Owen and Terry Kelly
                          1978 – Charlie Monk and Geoff Pusey
(1972–1974. Meetings held at Holker Street)
(1978. Meetings held at Park Road)

BELLE VUE

Northern League. 1929 (Resigned) 1930 (Winners) 1931 (Winners)
National League. 1932 (3rd) 1933 (Winners) 1934 (Winners) 1935 (Winners) 1936 (Winners) 1937 (4th) 1938 (5th) 1939 (Unfin) 1946 (2nd) 1947 (2nd) 1948 (5th) 1949 (2nd) 1950 (2nd) 1951 (2nd) 1952 (6th) 1953 (8th) 1954 (7th) 1955 (2nd) 1956 (5th) 1957 (2nd) 1958 (5th) 1959 (9th) 1960 (2nd) 1961 (4th) 1962 (4th) 1963 (Winners) 1964 (4th)
British League. Div. 1. 1965 (14th) 1966 (13th) 1967 (16th) 1968 (10th) 1969 (2nd) 1970 (Winners) 1971 (Winners) 1972 (Winners) 1973 (6th) 1974 (2nd) 1975 (2nd) 1976 (2nd) 1977 (5th) 1978 (2nd)

Leading Riders: 1929 – Frank Varey and Arthur Franklyn
                          1930 – Frank Varey and Eric Langton
                          1931 – Frank Varey and Eric Langton
                          1932 – Eric Langton and Frank Varey
                          1933 – Eric Langton and Bill Kitchen
                          1934 – Eric Langton and Bill Kitchen
                          1935 – Eric Langton and Max Grosskreutz
                          1936 – Max Grosskreutz and Eric Langton
                          1937 – Eric Langton and Bill Kitchen
                          1938 – Bill Kitchen and Frank Varey
                          1939 – Bill Kitchen and Eric Langton
                          1946 – Jack Parker and Eric Langton
                          1947 – Jack Parker and Dent Oliver
                          1948 – Jack Parker and Louis Lawson
                          1949 – Jack Parker and Dent Oliver
                          1950 – Jack Parker and Louis Lawson
                          1951 – Jack Parker and Louis Lawson
                          1952 – Ken Sharples and Henry Long
                          1953 – Ken Sharples and Ron Johnston
                          1954 – Ron Johnston and Peter Craven
                          1955 – Peter Craven and Ken Sharples
                          1956 – Peter Craven and Dick Fisher
                          1957 – Peter Craven and Ron Johnston

1958 – Peter Craven and Ron Johnston
1959 – Peter Craven and Ron Johnston
1960 – Peter Craven and Ron Johnston
1961 – Peter Craven and Ron Johnston
1962 – Peter Craven and Soren Sjosten
1963 – Peter Craven and Dick Fisher
1964 – Soren Sjosten and Dick Fisher
1965 – Cyril Maidment and Dick Fisher
1966 – Cyril Maidment and Sandor Levai
1967 – Cyril Maidment and Ove Fundin/Soren Sjosten
1968 – Soren Sjosten and Tommy Roper
1969 – Ivan Mauger and Soren Sjosten
1970 – Ivan Mauger and Soren Sjosten
1971 – Ivan Mauger and Soren Sjosten
1972 – Ivan Mauger and Soren Sjosten
1973 – Chris Pusey and Soren Sjosten
1974 – Peter Collins and Soren Sjosten
1975 – Peter Collins and Chris Morton
1976 – Peter Collins and Chris Morton
1977 – Peter Collins and Chris Morton
1978 – Peter Collins and Chris Morton

BERWICK

British League. Div. 2. 1968 (10) 1969 (14) 1970 (16) 1971 (8) 1972 (14th) 1973 (17th) 1974 (12th)
New National League. 1975 (7th) 1976 (10th) 1977 (18th) 1978 (11th)

Leading Riders:
1968 – Roy Williams and Bill McMillan
1969 – Maury Robinson and Mark Hall
1970 – Maury Robinson and Peter Kelly
1971 – Doug Wyer and Maury Robinson
1972 – Andy Meldrum and Jim Gallacher
1973 – Doug Templeton and Willie Templeton
1974 – Willie Templeton and Graham Jones
1975 – Dave Gifford and Graham Jones
1976 – Graham Jones and Dave Gifford
1977 – Graham Jones and Robin Adlington
1978 – Graham Jones and Roger Wright

BIRMINGHAM (Perry Barr)

Southern League. 1929 (9th)
Northern League. 1946 (4th)
National League. Div. 2. 1947 (4th) 1948 (2nd) **Div. 1.** 1949 (7th) 1950 (8th) 1951 (5th) 1952 (2nd) 1953 (3rd)
1954 (8th) 1955 (5th) 1956 (3rd) 1957 (Withdrew)
British League. Div. 2. 1971 (11th) 1972 (6th) 1973 (5th) 1974 (Winners) 1975 (Winners) **Div. 1.** 1976 (18th)
1977 (18th) 1978 (18th)

Leading Riders:
1929 – Wally Lloyd and Geoff Siddaway
1946 – Tiger Hart and Stan Dell
1947 – Stan Dell and Bob Lovell
1948 – Graham Warren and Stan Dell
1949 – Graham Warren and Wilbur Lamoreaux
1950 – Graham Warren and Geoff Bennett
1951 – Alan Hunt and Ron Mountford
1952 – Alan Hunt and Ron Mountford
1953 – Alan Hunt and Graham Warren
1954 – Alan Hunt and Ron Mountford
1955 – Alan Hunt and Ron Mountford
1956 – Alan Hunt and Doug Davies
1957 – Dan Forsberg and Nigel Boocock
1971 – George Major and Terry Shearer

110

1972 – Arthur Browning and Pete Bailey
1973 – Arthur Browning and Ted Howgego
1974 – Phil Herne and Arthur Browning
1975 – Arthur Browning and Alan Grahame
1976 – Gary Middleton and Soren Sjosten
1977 – Ray Wilson and Alan Grahame
1978 – Phil Herne and Ray Wilson

(1929–1957 Meetings held at Alexander Sports Ground)
(1971–1978 Meetings held at Greyhound Stadium)

BIRMINGHAM (Hall Green)

Southern League. 1929 (Withdrew) 1930 (5th)
National League. 1934 (7th). **Div. 2.** 1937 (6th) 1938 (8th)

Leading Riders:
1929 – Cyril Taft and Harry Taft
1930 – Harry Taft and Bunny Wilcox
1934 – Jack Ormston and Les Wotton
1937 – Les Bowden and Tiger Hart
1938 – Tiger Hart and Steve Langton

BOSTON

British League. Div. 2. 1970 (13th) 1971 (4th) 1972 (2nd) 1973 (Winners) 1974 (3rd)
New National League. 1975 (5th) 1976 (12th) 1977 (7th) 1978 (17th)

Leading Riders:
1970 – Ian Turner and Arthur Price
1971 – Arthur Price and Jim Ryman
1972 – Arthur Price and Jim Ryman
1973 – Carl Glover and Arthur Price
1974 – Carl Glover and Jim Ryman
1975 – Michael Lee and Bruce Forrester
1976 – Robert Hollingworth and Billy Burton
1977 – Robert Hollingworth and Carl Glover
1978 – Gary Gugliemi and Tony Boyle

BRISTOL

National League. Div. 2. 1936 (2nd) 1937 (Winners). **Div. 1.** 1938 (7th) **Div. 2.** 1939 (Unfinished)
National League. Div. 2. 1947 (6th) 1948 (Winners) 1949 (Winners) **Div. 1.** 1950 (7th) 1951 (6th) 1952 (8th) 1953 (9th) **Div. 2.** 1954 (Winners) 1955 (Withdrew).
Provincial League. 1960 (3rd)
British League. 1977 (12th) 1978 (9th)

Leading Riders:
1936 – Eric Collins and Harry Shepherd
1937 – Bill Rogers and Harry Shepherd
1938 – Cordy Milne and Vic Dulgan
1939 – Jeff Lloyd and Harry Shepherd
1947 – Mike Beddoe and Jack Mountford
1948 – Fred Tuck and Billy Hole
1949 – Billy Hole and Jack Mountford
1950 – Billy Hole and Dick Bradley
1951 – Geoff Pymar and Dick Bradley
1952 – Dick Bradley and Chris Boss
1953 – Olle Nygren and Dick Bradley
1954 – Dick Bradley and Jack Unstead
1955 – Dick Bradley and Jack Unstead
1960 – Johnnie Hole and Trevor Redmond
1977 – Phil Crump and Phil Herne
1978 – Phil Crump and Steve Gresham

(1936–1960. Meetings held at Knowle)
(1977–1978. Meetings held at Eastville)

Four stalwart members of the Belle Vue 'invincibles' 1933–36. Left to right: Eric Langton, Max Grosskreutz, Oliver Langton, Frank Varey

Odsal 1949. Left to right: Jack Biggs, Norman Price, Bob Lovell, Eric Langton (Manager), Oliver Hart, Eddie Rigg, Ernie Price, Joe Abbott and Ron Clarke (on machine)

Clapton in 1933. Riders left to right are Arthur Westwood, Norman Parker, John Deeley, Jack Parker (on bike), Wally Lloyd, Phil Bishop and Billy Dallinson

112

Presentation of the Coventry team in 1930. Riders left to right are: Arthur (Tiny) Tims, Lew Lancaster, Bill Stanley, Jack Parker (in hat), Norman Parker and Tom Farndon

CRYSTAL PALACE SPEEDWAY,
Southern League Team.

The Crystal Palace speedway team in 1929 (T.H. Everitt)

Hackney – 1937.
L to R: George Greenwood, Morian Hansen, Ted Bravery, Dick Case (on machine) George Wilks, Bill Clibbett, Vic Duggan, Cordy Milne, Frank Evans (Manager)

113

CANTERBURY

British League. Div. 2. 1968 (7th) 1969 (6th) 1970 (Winners) 1971 (14th) 1972 (13th) 1973 (15th) 1974 (10th)
New National League. 1975 (10th) 1976 (4th) 1977 (4th) 1978 (Winners)

Leading Riders:
    1968 – Barry Crowson and Peter Murray
    1969 – Peter Murray and Martyn Piddock
    1970 – Graeme Smith and Barry Crowson
    1971 – Ross Gilbertson and Graham Banks
    1972 – Ross Gilbertson and Graham Banks
    1973 – Barney Kennett and Peter Murray
    1974 – Trevor Jones and Ted Hubbard
    1975 – Les Rumsey and Dave Gooderham
    1976 – Graham Banks and Steve Koppe
    1977 – Steve Koppe and Graham Banks
    1978 – Les Rumsey and Steve Koppe

COVENTRY

Southern League. 1929 (3rd) 1930 (6th) 1931 (10th)
National League. 1932 (7th) 1933 (7th)
National League. Div. 3. 1948 (8th) **Div. 2.** 1949 (12th) 1950 (4th) 1951 (4th) 1952 (2nd) 1953 (Winners) 1954 (8th) 1955 (2nd) 1956 (5th) **Div. 1.** 1957 (8th) 1958 (7th) 1959 (3rd) 1960 (9th) 1961 (3rd) 1962 (3rd) 1963 (4th) 1964 (2nd)
British League. 1965 (3rd) 1966 (2nd) 1967 (2nd) 1968 (Winners) 1969 (14th) 1970 (3rd) 1971 (3rd) 1972 (10th) 1973 (15th) 1974 (15th) 1975 (16th) 1976 (4th) 1977 (8th) 1978 (Winners)

Leading Riders:
    1929 – Jack Parker and Tom Farndon
    1930 – Jack Parker and Tom Farndon
    1931 – Syd Jackson and Arthur Tims
    1932 – Syd Jackson and Stew Fairbairn
    1933 – Dick Case and Stan Greatrex
    1948 – Vic Emms and Bob Fletcher
    1949 – Bob Fletcher and Bert Lacey
    1950 – Les Hewitt and Stan Williams
    1951 – Les Hewitt and Bob Fletcher
    1952 – Vic Emms and Les Hewitt
    1953 – Charlie New and Les Hewitt
    1954 – Charlie New and Tommy Miller
    1955 – Bob Mark and Tommy Miller
    1956 – Bob Mark and Charlie New
    1957 – Ron Mountford and Peo Soderman
    1958 – Jack Young and Arthur Forrest
    1959 – Nigel Boocock and Arthur Forrest
    1960 – Jack Young and Nigel Boocock
    1961 – Jack Young and Nigel Boocock
    1962 – Ron Mountford and Ken McKinlay
    1963 – Nigel Boocock and Ken McKinlay
    1964 – Nigel Boocock and Ken McKinlay
    1965 – Nigel Boocock and Ron Mountford
    1966 – Nigel Boocock and Ron Mountford
    1967 – Nigel Boocock and Ron Mountford
    1968 – Nigel Boocock and Antonin Kasper
    1969 – Nigel Boocock and Antonin Kasper
    1970 – Nigel Boocock and Ken McKinlay
    1971 – Nigel Boocock and Tony Lomas
    1972 – Nigel Boocock and Tony Lomas
    1973 – Nigel Boocock and Gary Middleton
    1974 – Nigel Boocock and John Harrhy

1975 – Bob Valentine and Nigel Boocock
1976 – Ole Olson and Mitch Shirra
1977 – Ole Olsen and Mitch Shirra
1978 – Ole Olsen and Mitch Shirra

CRADLEY

National League. Div. 3. 1947 (2nd) 1948 (2nd) **Div. 2.** 1949 (4th) 1950 (3rd) 1951 (15th) 1952 (4th)
Provincial League. 1960 (6th) 1961 (4th) 1962 (8th) 1963 (9th) 1964 (10th)
British League. 1965 (16th) 1966 (19th) 1967 (18th) 1968 (14th) 1969 (7th) 1970 (15th) 1971 (18th) 1972 (16th) 1973 (18th) 1974 (13th) 1975 (11th) 1976 (9th) 1977 (7th) 1978 (5th)

Leading Riders:
1947 – Geoff Bennett and Les Beaumont
1948 – Les Beaumont and Gil Craven
1949 – Alan Hunt and Eric Williams
1950 – Alan Hunt and Eric Boothroyd
1951 – Gil Craven and Phil Malpass
1952 – Harry Bastable and Brian Shepherd
1960 – Eric Eadon and Harry Bastable
1961 – Ivor Brown and Harry Bastable
1962 – Ivor Brown and Harry Bastable
1963 – Ivor Brown and John Hart
1964 – Ivor Brown and John Hart
1965 – Ivor Brown and John Hart
1966 – Ivor Brown and Chris Julian
1967 – Ivor Brown and Brian Brett
1968 – Roy Trigg and Bob Andrews
1969 – Roy Trigg and Bernt Persson
1970 – Bernt Persson and Roy Trigg
1971 – Bernt Persson and Bob Andrews
1972 – Bernt Persson and Bob Andrews
1973 – Bernt Persson and Howard Cole
1974 – John Boulger and Howard Cole
1975 – John Boulger and Bernt Persson
1976 – John Boulger and Bruce Cribb
1977 – Anders Michanek and Bernt Persson
1978 – Steve Bastable and Bruce Penhall

CRAYFORD

British League. Div. 2. 1968 (6th) 1969 (4th) 1970 (14th)
New National League. 1975 (8th) 1976 (6th) 1977 (10th) 1978 (10th)

Leading Riders:
1968 – Mick Handley and Tony Childs
1969 – Geoff Ambrose and Arch Wilkinson
1970 – Arch Wilkinson and Tony Childs
1975 – Laurie Etheridge and Alan Sage
1976 – Laurie Etheridge and Alan Sage
1977 – Laurie Etheridge and Alan Sage
1978 – Laurie Etheridge and Alan Sage

EASTBOURNE

National League. Div. 3. 1947 (Winners)
Southern Area League. 1954 (5th) 1955 (4th) 1956 (2nd) 1957 (2nd) 1959 (Winners)
British League. Div. 2. 1969 (8th) 1970 (2nd) 1971 (Winners) 1972 (5th) 1973 (3rd) 1974 (2nd)
New National League. 1975 (4th) 1976 (8th) 1977 (Winners) 1978 (4th)

Leading Riders:
1947 – Basil Harris and Wally Green
1954 – Dan English and Johnny Fry
1955 – Merv Hannam and Wally Willson
1956 – Jim Heard and Leo McAuliffe
1957 – Frank Bettis and Jim Heard

Harringay 1948. Left to right: Steve Ison, Ray Duggan, Lloyd Goffe, Vic Duggan (Captain), Jimmy Grant, Jack Arnfield and Frank Dolan

Lea Bridge 1931

Liverpool 1936

116

Long Eaton 1951 (Ray Bennett)

Middlesbrough, Northern League champions 1946. Riders are: Kid Curtis, Eddie Pye, Len Tupling, Wilf Plant, Tip Mills, Geoff Godwin, Frank Hodgson, Jack Hodgson and Jack Gordon (Middlesbrough Evening Gazette)

New Cross during their first season in 1934. Left to right: Harry Shepherd, Roy Dook, Stan Greatrex, George Newton (back row), Joe Francis, Tom Farndon, Ron Johnson and Nobby Key (front row) with promoter Fred Mockford (centre)
(T.H. Everitt)

1959 – Colin Gooddy and Gil Goldfinch
1969 – Barry Crowson and Reg Trott
1970 – Dave Jessup and Derek Cook
1971 – Malcolm Ballard and Gordon Kennett
1972 – Malcolm Ballard and Gordon Kennett
1973 – Bobby McNeil and Ross Gilbertson
1974 – Bobby McNeil and Trevor Geer
1975 – Paul Gachet and Neil Middleditch
1976 – Steve Weatherley and Eric Dugard
1977 – Colin Richardson and Mike Sampson
1978 – Mike Sampson and Dave Kennett

EDINBURGH

Northern League. 1930 (Unfin)
National League. Div. 2. 1948 (9th) 1949 (5th) 1950 (8th) 1951 (3rd) 1952 (6th) 1953 (5th) 1954 (Withdrew)
Provincial League. 1960 (8th) 1961 (6th) 1962 (5th) 1963 (8th) 1964 (5th)
British League. 1965 (17th) 1966 (12th) 1967 (4th)
New National League. 1977 (15th) 1978 (15th)

Leading Riders:
1930 – Drew McQueen and Syd Parsons
1948 – Dick Campbell and Bill Maddern
1949 – Jack Young and Dick Campbell
1950 – Jack Young and Dick Campbell
1951 – Jack Young and Dick Campbell
1952 – Don Cuppleditch and Dick Campbell
1953 – Don Cuppleditch and Dick Campbell
1954 – Don Cuppleditch and Dick Campbell
1960 – Doug Templeton and Willie Templeton
1961 – Doug Templeton and Dick Campbell
1962 – Doug Templeton and Wayne Briggs
1963 – George Hunter and Doug Templeton
1964 – George Hunter and Doug Templeton
1965 – George Hunter and Doug Templeton
1966 – George Hunter and Bengt Jansson
1967 – Bernt Persson and Reidar Eide
1977 – Bert Harkins and Jack Millen
1978 – Rob Hollingworth and Bert Harkins

(1930. Meetings held at Marine Gardens)
(1948–1967. Meetings held at Meadowbank)
(1977–1978. Meetings held at Powderhall)

ELLESMERE PORT

British League. Div. 2. 1972 (15th) 1973 (14th) 1974 (14th)
New National League. 1975 (9th) 1976 (2nd) 1977 (3rd) 1978 (5th)

Leading Riders:
1972 – Paul Tyrer and Graham Drury
1973 – Graham Drury and Paul O'Neill
1974 – Graham Drury and Colin Goad
1975 – John Jackson and Colin Goad
1976 – John Jackson and Chris Turner
1977 – John Jackson and Steve Finch
1978 – John Jackson and Steve Finch

EXETER

National League. Div. 3. 1947 (4th) 1948 (Winners) 1949 (7th) 1950 (7th) 1951 (2nd)
Southern League. 1952 (5th) 1953 (Winners)
National League. Div. 2. 1954 (6th) 1955 (9th)
Provincial League. 1961 (8th) 1962 (3rd) 1963 (7th) 1964 (6th)

British League. 1965 (9th) 1966 (10th) 1967 (15th) 1968 (3rd) 1969 (12th) 1970 (10th) 1971 (15th) 1972 (11th) 1973 (8th) 1974 (Winners) 1975 (4th) 1976 (3rd) 1977 (2nd) 1978 (7th)

Leading Riders:
1947 – Cyril Roger and Don Hardy
1948 – Cyril Roger and Bert Roger
1949 – Norman Clay and Don Hardy
1950 – Don Hardy and Hugh Geddes
1951 – Bob Roger and Don Hardy
1952 – Goog Hoskin and Don Hardy
1953 – Goog Hoskin and Jack Geran
1954 – Jack Geran and Goog Hoskin
1955 – Jack Geran and Neil Street
1961 – Pete Lansdale and Len Silver
1962 – Len Silver and Pete Lansdale
1963 – Len Silver and Cliff Cox
1964 – Jimmy Squibb and Alan Cowland
1965 – Colin Gooddy and Jimmy Squibb
1966 – Tommy Sweetman and Neil Street
1967 – Gunnar Malmqvist and Wayne Briggs
1968 – Martin Ashby and Wayne Briggs
1969 – Martin Ashby and Jan Holub
1970 – Martin Ashby and Bruce Cribb
1971 – Bruce Cribb and Bob Kilby
1972 – Bob Kilby and Edgar Stangeland
1973 – Ivan Mauger and Tony Lomas
1974 – Ivan Mauger and Scott Autrey
1975 – Ivan Mauger and Scott Autrey
1976 – Ivan Mauger and Scott Autrey
1977 – Ivan Mauger and Scott Autrey
1978 – Scott Autrey and Reidar Eide

GLASGOW (White City)

Northern League. 1930 (Unfin) 1931 (Unfin)
Northern League. 1946 (6th)
National League. Div. 2. 1947 (8th) 1948 (6th) 1949 (8th) 1950 (2nd) 1951 (10th) 1952 (5th) 1953 (4th) 1954 (Withdrew)
Provincial League. 1964 (12th)
British League. 1965 (13th) 1966 (8th) 1967 (13th) 1968 (19th)

Leading Riders:
1930 – Col Stewart and Billy Galloway
1931 – Drew McQueen and Norrie Isbister
1946 – Will Lowther and Joe Crowther
1947 – Will Lowther and Joe Crowther
1948 – Joe Crowther and Will Lowther
1949 – Junior Bainbridge and Will Lowther
1950 – Tommy Miller and Junior Bainbridge
1951 – Tommy Miller and Junior Bainbridge
1952 – Tommy Miller and Ken McKinlay
1953 – Tommy Miller and Ken McKinlay
1954 – Ken McKinlay and Bob Sharp
1964 – Charlie Monk and Maury Mattingley
1965 – Charlie Monk and Bluey Scott
1966 – Charlie Monk and Alf Wells
1967 – Charlie Monk and Bo Josefsson
1968 – Jim McMillan and Oyvind Berg

GLASGOW (Hampden Park)

British League. Div. 1. 1969 (8th) 1970 (8th) 1971 (16th) 1972 (14th)

Leading Riders:
1969 – Jim McMillan and Charlie Monk
1970 – Jim McMillan and Charlie Monk

1971 – Jim McMillan and George Hunter
1972 – Jim McMillan and Bobby Beaton

GLASGOW (Blantyre)

New National League. 1977 (11th) 1978 (9th)

Leading Riders:
1977 – Brian Collins and Mick McKeon
1978 – Steve Lawson and Merv Janke

GLASGOW (Ashfield)

National League. Div. 2. 1949 (11th) 1950 (11th) 1951 (8th) 1952 (7th)

Leading Riders:
1949 – Ken Le Breton and Merv Harding
1950 – Ken Le Breton and Merv Harding
1951 – Merv Harding and Bruce Semmens
1952 – Bruce Semmens and Willie Wilson

HACKNEY

National League. 1935 (5th) 1936 (4th) 1937 (5th) **Div. 2.** 1938 (Winners) 1939 (Unfin)
Provincial League. 1963 (10th) 1964 (2nd)
British League. 1965 (8th) 1966 (14th) 1967 (5th) 1968 (2nd) 1969 (19th) 1970 (11th) 1971 (7th) 1972 (8th)
1973 (16th) 1974 (9th) 1975 (17th) 1976 (7th) 1977 (16th) 1978 (19th)

Leading Riders:
1935 – Dick Case and Dusty Haigh
1936 – Dick Case and Morian Hansen
1937 – Cordy Milne and Morian Hansen
1938 – Frank Hodgson and Doug Wells
1939 – Frank Hodgson and Doug Wells
1963 – Norman Hunter and Trevor Hedge
1964 – Colin Pratt and Roy Trigg
1965 – Gerry Jackson and Colin Pratt
1966 – Colin Pratt and Roy Trigg
1967 – Bengt Jansson and Colin Pratt
1968 – Colin Pratt and Bengt Jansson
1969 – Colin Pratt and Gary Middleton
1970 – Bengt Jansson and Gary Middleton
1971 – Bengt Jansson and Gary Middleton
1972 – Bengt Jansson and Barry Thomas
1973 – Bengt Jansson and Barry Thomas
1974 – Dag Lovaas and Barry Thomas
1975 – Dave Morton and Barry Thomas
1976 – Dave Morton and Zenon Plech
1977 – Barry Thomas and Keith White
1978 – Finn Thomsen and Keith White

HALIFAX (The Shay)

National League. Div. 3. 1949 (4th) **Div. 2.** 1950 (6th) 1951 (6th)
British League. 1965 (5th) 1966 (Winners) 1967 (7th) 1968 (7th) 1969 (4th) 1970 (6th) 1971 (14th) 1972
(12th) 1973 (9th) 1974 (7th) 1975 (10th) 1976 (15th) 1977 (17th) 1978 (12th)

Leading Riders:
1949 – Vic Emms and Arthur Forrest
1950 – Arthur Forrest and Vic Emms
1951 – Arthur Forrest and Vic Emms
1965 – Eric Boocock and Dave Younghusband
1966 – Eric Boocock and Eric Boothroyd
1967 – Eric Boocock and Dave Younghusband
1968 – Eric Boocock and Dave Younghusband
1969 – Eric Boocock and Dave Younghusband
1970 – Eric Boocock and Les Sharpe
1971 – Eric Boocock and Dave Younghusband

1972 – Eric Boocock and Gote Nordin
1973 – Eric Boocock and John Titman
1974 – Eric Boocock and Rick France
1975 – Chris Pusey and Rick France
1976 – Chris Pusey and Henny Kroeze
1977 – Chris Pusey and Henny Kroeze
1978 – Ian Cartwright and Mike Lohmann

HALIFAX (Thrum Hall)

Northern League. 1929 (3rd)

Leading Riders: 1929 – George Corney and Dusty Haigh

HULL

National League. Div. 3. 1948 (9th) 1949 (Withdrew)
British League. Div. 2. 1971 (6th) 1972 (8th) 1973 (12th) **Div. 1.** 1974 (16th) 1975 (14th) 1976 (12th) 1977 (14th) 1978 (3rd)

Leading Riders: 1948 – Mick Mitchell and George Craig
1949 – Mick Mitchell and Bob Baker
1971 – Reg Wilson and Tony Childs
1972 – Tony Childs and Dave Mills
1973 – Dave Mills and Tony Childs
1974 – Jim McMillan and Bobby Beaton
1975 – Jim McMillan and Bobby Beaton
1976 – Barry Briggs and Bobby Beaton
1977 – Graham Drury and Bobby Beaton
1978 – Ivan Mauger and Joe Owen

(1948–49. Meetings held at Hedon Stadium)
(1971–77. Meetings held at The Boulevard)

IPSWICH

Southern League. 1952 (8th) 1953 (3rd)
National League. Div. 2. 1954 (5th) 1955 (6th) 1956 (4th) **Div. 1.** 1957 (10th) 1958 (10th)
Southern Area League. 1959 (5th)
National League. Div. 1. 1960 (4th) 1961 (6th) 1962 (Withdrew)
British League. Div. 2. 1969 (11th) 1970 (6th) 1971 (3rd) **Div. 1.** 1972 (6th) 1973 (5th) 1974 (3rd) 1975 (Winners) 1976 (Winners) 1977 (4th) 1978 (6th)

Leading Riders: 1952 – Sid Clark and Harold McNaughton
1953 – Sid Clark and Harold McNaughton
1954 – Junior Bainbridge and Bert Edwards
1955 – Bert Edwards and Junior Bainbridge
1956 – Bob Sharp and Bert Edwards
1957 – Peter Moore and Cyril Roger
1958 – Peter Moore and Ray Cresp
1959 – Gil Goldfinch and Jim Heard
1960 – Peter Moore and Ray Cresp
1961 – Peter Moore and Ray Cresp
1962 – Peter Moore and Colin Gooddy
1969 – John Harrhy and Pete Bailey
1970 – John Harrhy and John Louis
1971 – John Louis and Tony Davey
1972 – John Louis and Olle Nygren
1973 – John Louis and Tony Davey
1974 – John Louis and Billy Sanders
1975 – John Louis and Billy Sanders
1976 – John Louis and Billy Sanders
1977 – Billy Sanders and John Louis
1978 – Billy Sanders and Tony Davey

KINGS LYNN

British League. 1966 (16th) 1967 (19th) 1968 (18th) 1969 (9th) 1970 (12th) 1971 (13th) 1972 (3rd) 1973 (3rd) 1974 (5th) 1975 (12th) 1976 (14th) 1977 (6th) 1978 (13th)

Leading Riders:
1966 – Terry Betts and Peter Moore
1967 – Terry Betts and David Crane
1968 – Terry Betts and Malcolm Simmons
1969 – Terry Betts and Malcolm Simmons
1970 – Terry Betts and Howard Cole
1971 – Terry Betts and Malcolm Simmons
1972 – Terry Betts and Howard Cole
1973 – Malcolm Simmon and Terry Betts
1974 – Terry Betts and Malcolm Simmons
1975 – Terry Betts and Ian Turner
1976 – Terry Betts and Michael Lee
1977 – Michael Lee and Terry Betts
1978 – Michael Lee and Terry Betts

LEICESTER

Northern League. 1929 (5th)
Southern League. 1930 (10th) 1931 (Withdrew)
National League. Div. 2. 1937 (Withdrew)
National League. Div. 3. 1949 (10th) 1950 (3rd) **Div. 2.** 1951 (2nd) 1952 (3rd) 1953 (8th) 1954 (4th) 1955 (7th) 1956 (6th) **Div. 1.** 1957 (5th) 1958 (4th) 1959 (2nd) 1960 (6th) 1961 (10th)
Provincial League. 1962 (12th)
British League. Div. 1. 1968 (12th) 1969 (5th) 1970 (4th) 1971 (2nd) 1972 (5th) 1973 (4th) 1974 (10th) 1975 (8th) 1976 (19th) 1977 (19th) 1978 (11th)

Leading Riders:
1929 – Sid Jackson and Billy Ellmore
1930 – Squib Burton and Sid Jackson
1931 – Squib Burton and Alby Taylor
1937 – Lloyd Goffe and Danny Lee
1949 – Vic Pitcher and Cyril Page
1950 – Harwood Pike and Jock Grierson
1951 – Len Williams and Lionel Benson
1952 – Len Williams and Lionel Benson
1953 – Len Williams and Charlie Barsby
1954 – Ken McKinlay and Jock Grierson
1955 – Ken McKinlay and Gordon MacGregor
1956 – Ken McKinlay and Gordon MacGregor
1957 – Ken McKinlay and Jack Geran
1958 – Ken McKinlay and Jack Geran
1959 – Ken McKinlay and Jack Geran
1960 – Ken McKinlay and Stefan Kwoczala
1961 – Ken McKinlay and Pawel Waloszek
1962 – Norman Hunter and Rick France
1968 – Anders Michanek and Ray Wilson
1969 – Ray Wilson and John Boulger
1970 – Ray Wilson and John Boulger
1971 – Ray Wilson and John Boulger
1972 – Ray Wilson and John Boulger
1973 – John Boulger and Ray Wilson
1974 – Dave Jessup and Ray Wilson
1975 – Dave Jessup and Ray Wilson
1976 – Ray Wilson and Reidar Eide
1977 – Ila Teromaa and John Boulger
1978 – Ila Teromaa and John Titman

LEICESTER SUPER

Northern League. 1930 (Unfin) 1931 (Unfin)

Leading Riders:
1930 – Hal Herbert and Fred Wilkinson
1931 – Arthur Jervis and Fred Wilkinson

MILDENHALL

New National League. 1975 (19th) 1976 (13th) 1977 (8th) 1978 (12th)

Leading Riders:
1975 – Bob Coles and Chris Julian
1976 – Bob Coles and Kevin Jolly
1977 – Bob Coles and Trevor Jones
1978 – Ray Bales and Bob Coles

MILTON KEYNES

National League. 1978 (16th)

Leading Riders:
Bob Humphreys and Derek Harrison

NEWCASTLE (Brough Park)

Northern League. 1929 (9th)
National League. Div. 2. 1938 (6th) 1939 (Unfin)
Northern League. 1946 (5th)
National League. Div. 2. 1947 (5th) 1948 (7th) 1949 (10th)1950 (13th) 1951 (16th)
Provincial League. 1961 (11th) 1962 (9th) 1963 (6th) 1964 (Winners)
British League. 1965 (12th) 1966 (5th) 1967 (10th) 1968 (5th) 1969 (13) 1970 (17th)
New National League. 1975 (2nd) 1976 (Winners) 1977 (6th) 1978 (2nd)

Leading Riders:
1929 – Walter Creasor and Gordon Byers
1938 – George Pepper and Rol Stobart
1939 – George Pepper and Rol Stobart
1946 – Jeff Lloyd and Norman Evans
1947 – Wilf Jay and Doug McLachlan
1948 – Wilf Jay and Norman Evans
1949 – Derek Close and Jack Hodgson
1950 – Derek Close and Frank Hodgson
1951 – Derek Close and Son Mitchell
1961 – Don Wilkinson and Gil Goldfinch
1962 – Brian Craven and Gil Goldfinch
1963 – Ivan Mauger and Brian Craven
1964 – Ivan Mauger and Bill Andrew
1965 – Brian Brett and Ivan Mauger
1966 – Ivan Mauger and Peter Kelly
1967 – Ivan Mauger and Ole Olsen
1968 – Ivan Mauger and Ole Olsen
1969 – Ole Olsen and Dave Gifford
1970 – Anders Michanek and George Hunter
1975 – Tom Owen and Joe Owen
1976 – Joe Owen and Tom Owen
1977 – Tom Owen and Robbie Blackadder
1978 – Tom Owen and Robbie Blackadder

NEWCASTLE (Gosforth)

Northern League. 1930 (Unfin)

Leading Riders:
1930 – Tiger Sanderson and Buzz Hibberd

The pre-war Norwich team managed
by Max Grosskreutz (fourth from left).
Captain Dick Wise is on the machine

A photograph taken at Oxford during
1940. Riders include Roy Dukes,
Geoff Godwin, Wilf Plant, Reg
Lamborne, Charlie Page, Ron Clarke,
Phil Hart and Arthur Flack

Plymouth 1932

124

BILL CLIBBETT, BERT SPENCER, BILL STANLEY,
 (1ST ON THE LEFT)
FRANK PEARCE, TED BRAVERY, JACK JACKSON.

Walthamstow in their first post-war season 1949. Riders left to right: Jim Boyd, Harold Bull, Bill Osborne, Dick Geary, Harry Edwards, Charlie May and Wilf Jay (on machine). Manager Wally Lloyd is on the extreme left

The great Wembley side that cleaned up everything in 1932 photographed with the National Trophy

Wimbledon 1947. Left to right: Cyril Brine, Dick Harris, George Saunders, Mike Erskine, Norman Parker and Lloyd Goffe (on bike), Archie Windmill and Les Wotton. Promoter Ronnie Greene is fourth from left

NEWPORT

Provincial League. 1964 (4th)
British League. 1965 (6th) 1966 (17th) 1967 (12th) 1968 (13th) 1969 (17th) 1970 (19th) 1971 (8th) 1972 (18th) 1973 (10th) 1974 (6th) 1975 (3rd) 1976 (8th)
New National League. 1977 (12th)

Leading Riders:
1964 – Dick Bradley and Peter Vandenberg
1965 – Jack Biggs and Dick Bradley
1966 – Gote Nordin and Jack Biggs
1967 – Torbjorn Harrysson and Jimmy Gooch
1968 – Torbjorn Harrysson and Jimmy Gooch
1969 – Sandor Levai and Norman Strachan
1970 – Sandor Levai and Bill Andrew
1971 – Sandor Levai and Tommy Johansson
1972 – Ronnie Genz and Tony Clarke
1973 – Reidar Eide and Graham Plant
1974 – Phil Crump and Reidar Eide
1975 – Phil Crump and Reidar Eide
1976 – Phil Crump and Phil Herne
1977 – Jim Brett and Brian Woodward
1978 –

OXFORD

National League. Div. 3. 1949 (13th) 1950 (Winners) **Div. 2.** 1951 (12th) 1952 (12th)
Southern League. 1953 (6th)
National League. Div. 2. 1954(7th) 1955 (4th) 1956 (7th) **Div. 1.** 1957 (9th) 1958 (8th) 1959 (7th) 1960 (3rd) 1961 (9th) 1962 (7th) 1963 (7th) 1964 (Winners)
British League. 1965 (4th) 1966 (15th) 1967 (14th) 1968 (15th) 1969 (15th) 1970 (13th) 1971 (17th) 1972 (17th) 1973 (11th) 1974 (16th) 1975 (7th)
New National League. 1976 (14th) 1977 (13th) 1978 (7th)

Leading Riders:
1949 – Dennis Gray and Bert Croucher
1950 – Pat Clarke and Bob McFarlane
1951 – Bill Osborne and Ernie Rawlins
1952 – Jim Gregory and Jim Boyd
1953 – Jim Boyd and Jim Gregory
1954 – Peter Robinson and Ronnie Genz
1955 – Bob Baker and Ronnie Genz
1956 – Ronnie Genz and Peter Robinson
1957 – Ronnie Genz and Jack Biggs
1958 – Gordon McGregor and Charlie New
1959 – Arne Pander and Gordon McGregor
1960 – Arne Pander and Ronnie Genz
1961 – Arne Pander and Ronnie Genz
1962 – Jack Geran and Alf Hagon
1963 – Jack Geran and Ronnie Genz
1964 – Ron How and Arne Pander
1965 – Ron How and Arne Pander
1966 – Arne Pander and Jimmy Gooch
1967 – Roy Trigg and Arne Pander
1968 – Ronnie Genz and Eddie Reeves
1969 – Eddie Reeves and Colin Gooddy
1970 – Hasse Holmqvist and Ronnie Genz
1971 – Oyvind Berg and Ken McKinlay
1972 – Gary Middleton and Oyvind Berg
1973 – Hasse Holmqvist and Bob Kilby
1974 – Bob Kilby and Gordon Kennett
1975 – Dag Lovaas and Gordon Kennett
1976 – Carl Askew and Brian Leonard
1977 – Martin Yeates and Phil Bass
1978 – George Hunter and Dave Shields

PETERBOROUGH

British League. Div. 2. 1970 (10th) 1971 (16th) 1972 (3rd) 1973 (4th) 1974 (8th)
New National League. 1975 (18th) 1976 (8th) 1977 (5th) 1978 (6th)

Leading Riders:
    1970 – Andy Ross and Richard Greer
    1971 – Richard Greer and Roy Carter
    1972 – Richard Greer and Roy Carter
    1973 – Richard Greer and John Davis
    1974 – Mike Lanham and Brian Clark
    1975 – Brian Clark and Russell Osborne
    1976 – Brian Clark and Tony Featherstone
    1977 – Andy Hines and Ian Clark
    1978 – Dave Gooderham and Andy Hines

POOLE

National League. Div. 3. 1948 (10th) 1949 (6th) 1950 (2nd) 1951 (Winners) **Div. 2.** 1952 (Winners) 1953 (2nd) 1954 (2nd) 1955 (Winners) **Div. 1** 1956 (6th) 1958 (9th) 1959 (6th)
Provincial League. 1960 (2nd) 1961 (Winners) 1962 (Winners) 1963 (3rd) 1964 (7th)
British League. 1965 (10th) 1966 (6th) 1967 (6th) 1968 (17th) 1969 (Winners) 1970 (5th) 1971 (11th) 1972 (7th) 1973 (14th) 1974 (14th) 1975 (15th) 1976 (10th) 1977 (10th) 1978 (10th)

Leading Riders:
    1948 – Joe Bowkis and Alan Chambers
    1949 – Alan Chambers and Cyril Quick
    1950 – Ken Middleditch and Cyril Quick
    1951 – Ken Middleditch and Terry Small
    1952 – Brian Crutcher and Ken Middleditch
    1953 – Ken Middleditch and Terry Small
    1954 – Ken Middleditch and Bill Holden
    1955 – Ken Middleditch and Bill Holden
    1956 – Jack Biggs and Cyril Roger
    1958 – Jack Biggs and Les McGillivray
    1959 – Ray Cresp and Jack Unstead
    1960 – Tony Lewis and Ross Gilbertson
    1961 – Ken Middleditch and Ross Gilbertson
    1962 – Geoff Mudge and Tony Lewis
    1963 – Ross Gilbertson and Geoff Mudge
    1964 – Geoff Mudge and Ross Gilbertson
    1965 – Ronnie Genz and Bill Andrew
    1966 – Bill Andrew and Ronnie Genz
    1967 – Gote Nordin and Geoff Mudge
    1968 – Bill Andrew and Geoff Mudge
    1969 – Pete Smith and Geoff Mudge
    1970 – Geoff Mudge and Gordon Guasco
    1971 – Reidar Eide and Odd Fossengen
    1972 – Christer Lofqvist and Pete Smith
    1973 – Christer Lofqvist and Pete Smith
    1974 – Eric Broadbelt and Pete Smith
    1975 – Malcolm Simmons and Eric Broadbelt
    1976 – Malcolm Simmons and Eric Broadbelt
    1977 – Malcolm Simmons and Christer Sjosten
    1978 – Malcolm Simmons and Neil Middleditch

READING

British League. Div. 2. 1968 (8th) 1969 (2nd) 1970 (9th) **Div. 1.** 1971 (6th) 1972 (2nd) 1973 (Winners) 1975 (6th) 1976 (6th) 1977 (3rd) 1978 (14th)

Leading Riders:
    1968 – John Poyser and Vic White
    1969 – Mick Bell and Richard May
    1970 – Richard May and Mike Vernam
    1971 – Anders Michanek and Dag Lovaas

1972 – Anders Michanek and Dag Lovaas
1973 – Anders Michanek and Dag Lovaas
1975 – Anders Michanek and John Davis
1976 – Dave Jessup and John Davis
1977 – Dave Jessup and John Davis
1978 – Dave Jessup and John Davis

(1968–1973. Meetings held at Tilehurst)
(1975–1978. Meetings held at Smallmead)

RYE HOUSE

Southern Area League. 1954 (Winners) 1955 (Winners) 1956 (Winners) 1957 (4th) 1959 (4th).
British League. Div. 2. 1974 (16th)
New National League. 1975 (14th) 1976 (5th) 1977 (2nd) 1978 (3rd)

Leading Riders:
1954 – Vic Ridgeon and Jim Heard
1955 – Mike Broadbanks and Vic Ridgeon
1956 – Vic Ridgeon and Gerry King
1957 – Gerry King and Bobby Croombs
1959 – Tommy Sweetman and Ronnie Rolfe
1974 – Brian Foote and Clive Hitch
1975 – Brian Foote and Hugh Saunders
1976 – Ted Hubbard and Kelvin Mullarkey
1977 – Kelvin Mullarkey and Ted Hubbard
1978 – Ted Hubbard and Kelvin Mullarkey

SCUNTHORPE

British League. Div. 2. 1972 (17th) 1973 (16th) 1974 (18th)
New National League. 1975 (13th) 1976 (17th) 1977 (14th) 1978 (19th)

Leading Riders:
1972 – Brian Maxted and Terry Kelly
1973 – Ken McKinlay and Ian Hindle
1974 – Tony Childs and Ken McKinlay
1975 – Tony Childs and Keith Evans
1976 – Keith Evans and Andy Hines
1977 – Nicky Allott and Arthur Browning
1978 – Nicky Allot and John McNeill

SHEFFIELD

Northern League. 1929 (8th) 1930 (Unfin) 1931 (Unfin)
National League. 1932 (Withdrew) 1933 (8th) **Div. 2.** 1938 (7th) 1939 (Unfin)
Northern League. 1946 (2nd)
National League. Div. 2. 1947 (2nd) 1948 (4th) 1949 (2nd) 1950 (10th)
Provincial League. 1960 (4th) 1961 (7th) 1962 (7th) 1963 (4th) 1964 (8th)
British League. 1965 (11th) 1966 (11th) 1967 (9th) 1968 (4th) 1969 (6th) 1970 (7th) 1971 (4th) 1972 (4th)
1973 (2nd) 1974 (4th) 1975 (5th) 1976 (17th) 1977 (13th) 1978 (8th)

Leading Riders:
1929 – Clem Beckett and Smoky Stratton
1930 – Jack Chapman and Chun Moore
1931 – Dusty Haigh and Eric Blain
1932 – Squib Burton and Eric Blain
1933 – Squib Burton and Eric Blain
1938 – Billy Lamont and Ted Bravery
1939 – Ernie Evans and Stan Williams
1946 – Stan Williams and Tommy Allott
1947 – Tommy Bateman and Jack Bibby
1948 – Bruce Semmens and Tommy Bateman
1949 – Bruce Semmens and Stan Williams
1950 – Len Williams and Peter Orpwood
1960 – Tony Robinson and Jack Kitchen
1961 – Guy Allott and Clive Featherby

1962 – Guy Allott and Clive Featherby
1963 – Clive Featherby and Jack Kitchen
1964 – Clive Featherby and Jack Kitchen
1965 – Jack Kitchen and Clive Featherby
1966 – John Dews and Bob Paulson
1967 – John Hart and Bengt Larsson
1968 – Charlie Monk and Bengt Larsson
1969 – Jim Airey and Bengt Larsson
1970 – Jim Airey and Arnold Haley
1971 – Jim Airey and Arnold Haley
1972 – Reidar Eide and Arnold Haley
1973 – Bob Valentine and Arnold Haley
1974 – Bob Valentine and Reg Wilson
1975 – Doug Wyer and Arnold Haley
1976 – Doug Wyer and Reg Wilson
1977 – Doug Wyer and Reg Wilson
1978 – Doug Wyer and Reg Wilson

STOKE

National League. Div. 2. 1939 (Withdrew) **Div. 3.** 1947 (6th) 1948 (5th) 1949 (Winners) **Div. 2.** 1950 (14th) 1951 (9th) 1952 (10th) 1953 (9th)
Provincial League. 1960 (5th) 1961 (3rd) 1962 (4th) 1963 (2nd)
British League. Div. 2. 1973 (13th) 1974 (13th)
New National League. 1975 (3rd) 1976 (11th) 1977 (19th) 1978 (8th)

Leading Riders:
1939 – Ted Bravery and Oliver Hart
1947 – Dave Anderson and Vic Pitcher
1948 – Gil Blake and Les Jenkins
1949 – Ken Adams and Gil Blake
1950 – Brian Pritchett and Lindsay Mitchell
1951 – Ken Adams and Lindsay Mitchell
1952 – Ken Adams and Ron Peace
1953 – Ken Adams and Don Potter
1960 – Reg Fearman and Ray Harris
1961 – Brian Craven and Ken Adams
1962 – Eric Hockaday and Ken Adams
1963 – Colin Pratt and Peter Jarman
1973 – Mike Broadbanks and Geoff Pusey
1974 – Mike Broadbanks and Geoff Pusey
1975 – Alan Molyneux and Steve Bastable
1976 – Les Collins and Jack Millen
1977 – Stuart Mountford and Tim Nunan
1978 – Tony Lomas and John Harrhy

(1939–1953. Meetings held at Sun Street)
(1973–1978. Meetings held at Chesterton)

SWINDON

National League. Div. 3. 1949 (11th) 1950 (4th) 1951 (5th)
Southern League. 1952 (6th) 1953 (4th)
National League. Div. 2. 1954 (3rd) 1955 (8th) 1956 (Winners) **Div. 1.** 1957 (Winners) 1958 (6th) 1959 (8th) 1960 (10th) 1961 (5th) 1962 (6th) 1963 (5th) 1964 (5th)
British League. 1965 (15th) 1966 (3rd) 1967 (Winners) 1968 (11th) 1969 (10th) 1970 (16th) 1971 (5th) 1972 (15th) 1973 (13th) 1974 (12th) 1975 (18th) 1976 (5th) 1977 (11th) 1978 (16th)

Leading Riders:
1949 – Mick Mitchell and George Craig
1950 – High Geddes and Alex Gray
1951 – Buster Brown and Danny Malone
1952 – Frank Evans and Bob Jones
1953 – Ian Williams and Danny Malone
1954 – Bob Roger and Ian Williams

1955 – Bob Roger and Ian Williams
1956 – Ian Williams and Bob Roger
1957 – Bob Roger and George White
1958 – Mike Broadbanks and Ian Williams
1959 – Mike Broadbanks and George White
1960 – Mike Broadbanks and George White
1961 – Neil Street and Teo Teodorowicz
1962 – Mike Broadbanks and Peter Moore
1963 – Peter Moore and Mike Broadbanks
1964 – Barry Briggs and Mike Broadbanks
1965 – Barry Briggs and Mike Broadbanks
1966 – Barry Briggs and Mike Broadbanks
1967 – Barry Briggs and Martin Ashby
1968 – Barry Briggs and Mike Broadbanks
1969 – Barry Briggs and Bob Kilby
1970 – Barry Briggs and Bob Kilby
1971 – Barry Briggs and Martin Ashby
1972 – Barry Briggs and Martin Ashby
1973 – Martin Ashby and Norman Hunter
1974 – Martin Ashby and Edgar Stangeland
1975 – Martin Ashby and Bob Kilby
1976 – Martin Ashby and Bob Kilby
1977 – Martin Ashby and Bob Kilby
1978 – Bob Kilby and Jan Andersson

TEESSIDE/MIDDLESBROUGH

Northern League. 1929 (11th)
National League. Div. 2. 1939 (Withdrew)
Northern League. 1946 (Winners)
National League. Div. 2. 1947 (Winners) 1948 (3rd) 1978 (18th)
Provincial League. 1961 (10th) 1962 (11th) 1963 (11th) 1964 (9th)
British League. Div. 2. 1968 (3rd) 1969 (9th) 1970 (5th) 1971 (13th) 1972 (10th) 1973 (6th) 1974 (7th) 1975 (17th) 1976 (18th) 1977 (9th) 1978 (18th)

Leading Riders:
1929 – Norman Evans and Bronco Dixon
1939 – George Greenwood and Aub Lawson
1946 – Kid Curtis and Frank Hodgson
1947 – Frank Hodgson and Wilf Plant
1948 – Frank Hodgson and Jack Hodgson
1961 – Eric Boothroyd and Tommy Roper
1962 – Eric Boothroyd and Brian McKeown
1963 – Eric Boocock and Eric Boothroyd
1964 – Dave Younghusband and Eric Boocock
1968 – Allan Brown and Graham Plant
1969 – Terry Lee and Tom Leadbitter
1970 – Tom Leadbitter and Roger Mills
1971 – Bruce Forrester and Tim Swales
1972 – Roger Wright and Dave Durham
1973 – Bruce Forrester and Frank Auffret
1974 – Bruce Forrester and Dave Durham
1975 – Tom Leadbitter and Doug Underwood
1976 – Alan Emerson and Tom Leadbitter
1977 – Alan Emerson and Steve Wilcock
1978 – Nigel Close and Steve Wilcock

WEYMOUTH

National League. Div. 2. 1955 (Withdrew)
British League. Div. 2. 1968 (9th) 1974 (19th)
New National League. 1975 (20th) 1976 (15th) 1977 (17th) 1978 (13th)

Leading Riders:
1955 – Ern Brecknell and Ken Adams

130

1968 – Tony Lomas and Mike Vernam
1974 – Kelvin Mullarkey and Bob Hughes
1975 – Martin Yeates and Brian Woodward
1976 – Martin Yeates and Vic Harding
1977 – Danny Kennedy and Vic Harding
1978 – Danny Kennedy and Malcolm Shakespeare

WHITE CITY

Southern League. 1929 (7th)
British League. 1976 (13th) 1977 (Winners) 1978 (15th)

Leading Riders:
1929 – Colin Watson and Harold Crook
1976 – Gordon Kennett and Dag Lovaas
1977 – Gordon Kennett and Steve Weatherley
1978 – Gordon Kennett and Kal Niemi

WIMBLEDON

Southern League. 1929 (11th) 1930 (4th) 1931 (5th)
National League. 1932 (5th) 1933 (2nd) 1934 (5th) 1935 (7th) 1936 (5th) 1937 (7th) 1938 (4th) 1939 (Unfin)
1946 (4th) 1947 (3rd) 1948 (6th) 1949 (8th) 1950 (3rd) 1951 (3rd) 1952 (5th) 1953 (5th) 1954 (Winners)
1955 (Winners) 1956 (Winners) 1957 (3rd) 1958 (Winners) 1959 (Winners) 1960 (Winners) 1961 (Winners)
1962 (2nd) 1963 (3rd) 1964 (6th)
British League. 1965 (2nd) 1966 (4th) 1967 (11th) 1968 (9th) 1969 (3rd) 1970 (2nd) 1971 (10th) 1972 (13th)
1973 (12th) 1974 (8th) 1975 (9th) 1976 (16th) 1977 (9th) 1978 (4th)

Leading Riders:
1929 – Jim Kempster and Mart Seiffert
1930 – Jim Kempster and Dick Case
1931 – Dick Case and Vic Huxley
1932 – Vic Huxley and Dick Case
1933 – Vic Huxley and Claude Rye
1934 – Vic Huxley and Wal Phillips
1935 – Vic Huxley and Geoff Pymar
1936 – Vic Huxley and Wal Phillips
1937 – Wilbur Lamoreaux and Eric Collins
1938 – Wilbur Lamoreaux and Benny Kaufman
1939 – Wilbur Lamoreaux and Vic Duggan
1946 – Norman Parker and Oliver Hart
1947 – Norman Parker and Les Wotton
1948 – Norman Parker and Alec Statham
1949 – Norman Parker and Alex Statham
1950 – Norman Parker and Alec Statham
1951 – Ronnie Moore and Norman Parker
1952 – Ronnie Moore and Cyril Brine
1953 – Ronnie Moore and Geoff Mardon
1954 – Ronnie Moore and Geoff Mardon
1955 – Ronnie Moore and Barry Briggs
1956 – Barry Briggs and Ronnie Moore
1957 – Barry Briggs and Ron How
1958 – Barry Briggs and Ron How
1959 – Ronnie Moore and Peter Moore
1960 – Ronnie Moore and Ron How
1961 – Ronnie Moore and Ron How
1962 – Ronnie Moore and Ron How
1963 – Ron How and Sverre Harrfeldt
1964 – Gote Nordin and Sverre Harrfeldt
1965 – Olle Nygren and Reg Luckhurst
1966 – Olle Nygren and Trevor Hedge
1967 – Olle Nygren and Trevor Hedge
1968 – Olle Nygren and Trevor Hedge
1969 – Trevor Hedge and Ronnie Moore

1970 – Trevor Hedge and Ronnie Moore
1971 – Ronnie Moore and Trevor Hedge
1972 – Ronnie Moore and Trevor Hedge
1973 – Tommy Jansson and Trevor Hedge
1974 – Barry Briggs and Trevor Hedge
1975 – Tommy Jansson and Barry Briggs
1976 – Mick Hines and Edgar Stangeland
1977 – Edward Jancarz and Mick Hines
1978 – Larry Ross and Edward Jancarz

WOLVERHAMPTON

National League. Div. 3. 1951 (10th)
Southern League. 1952 (4th)
National League. Div. 2. 1953 (7th) 1954 (Withdrew)
Provincial League. 1961 (9th) 1962 (10th) 1963 (Winners) 1964 (3rd)
British League. 1965 (7th) 1966 (9th) 1967 (8th) 1968 (16th) 1969 (16th) 1970 (9th) 1971 (12th) 1972 (9th)
1973 (7th) 1974 (11th) 1975 (13th) 1976 (11th) 1977 (15th) 1978 (17th)

Leading Riders:
1951 – Roy Moreton and Jack Cunningham
1952 – Benny King and Cyril Quick
1953 – Brian Shepherd and Jim Tolley
1954 – Jim Tolley and Les Tolley
1961 – Graham Warren and Tommy Sweetman
1962 – Tommy Sweetman and Graham Warren
1963 – Tommy Sweetman and Maury Mattingley
1964 – Pete Jarman and Tommy Sweetman
1965 – Pete Jarman and Bob Andrews
1966 – Peter Vandenberg and Gordon Guasco
1967 – Jim Airey and Hasse Holmqvist
1968 – Hasse Holmqvist and Jim Airey
1969 – Norman Hunter and James Bond
1970 – Ole Olsen and Norman Hunter
1971 – Ole Olsen and Norman Hunter
1972 – Ole Olsen and Jan Simenson
1973 – Ole Olsen and George Hunter
1974 – Ole Olsen and George Hunter
1975 – Ole Olsen and George Hunter
1976 – Jim McMillan and Finn Thomsen
1977 – Jim McMillan and Finn Thomsen
1978 – Hans Nielsen and Dave Morton

WORKINGTON

British League. Div. 2. 1970 (11th) 1971 (15th) 1972 (7th) 1973 (2nd) 1974 (4th)
New National League. 1975 (6th) 1976 (3rd) 1977 (16th) 1978 (14th)

Leading Riders:
1970 – Bob Valentine and Malcolm Mackay
1971 – Malcolm Mackay and Taffy Owen
1972 – Taffy Owen and Lou Sansom
1973 – Lou Sansom and Malcolm Mackay
1974 – Mitch Graham and Malcolm Mackay
1975 – Lou Sansom and Taffy Owen
1976 – Lou Sansom and Steve Lawson
1977 – Steve Lawson and Brian Havelock
1978 – Arthur Price and Brian Havelock

Wimbledon's first championship win in 1954. Left to right: Ronnie Moore, Cyril Brine, Geoff Mardon, Cyril Maidment, Barry Briggs, Reg Trott, Don Perry, and Bill Longley

An informal group c.1960. Riders featured are Bob Andrews, Ken McKinlay, Peter Moore, Mike Broadbanks (back row), and Ron Mountford, Peter Craven and Nigel Boocock (front row)

Jim Kempster

Frank Arthur

Sprouts Elder

Colin Watson

Team champions

The Premier League Winners 1929–1978

The Tracks and the Men

| 1929 | **STAMFORD BRIDGE** | Southern League |

Gus Kuhn, Colin Ford, Wal Phillips, Ernie Maine, Nick Nicol, Fred Ralph, Bert Bolt, W.H.White, Les Blakeborough, Arthur Warwick, Bill Bragg

| 1929 | **LEEDS** | Northern League |

Eric Langton, Oliver Langton, George Greenwood, Arthur Atkinson, Alec Hill, Tommy Gamble, Billy Burrows, Roy Barrowclough, Harry Watson.

| 1930 | **WEMBLEY** | Southern League |

Colin Watson, George Greenwood, Jack Ormston, Harry Whitfield, Buster Frogley, Arthur Atkinson, Wally Kilmister, Norman Evans, Stan Catlett

| 1930 | **BELLE VUE** | Northern League |

Frank Varey, Arthur Franklyn, Eric Langton, Oliver Langton, Dusty Haigh, Bob Harrison, Bruce McCallum, Clem Cort

| 1931 | **WEMBLEY** | Southern League |

Colin Watson, Jack Ormston, George Greenwood, Harry Whitfield, Norman Evans, Lionel Van Praag, Buster Frogley, Wally Kilmister, Jack Jackson

| 1931 | **BELLE VUE** | Northern League |

Frank Varey, Eric Langton, Wally Hull, Bob Harrison, Oliver Langton, Len Woods, Chun Moore, Frank Burgess

| 1932 | **WEMBLEY** | National League |

Jack Ormston, Wally Kilmister, Ginger Lees, George Greenwood, Harry Whitfield, Norman Evans, Colin Watson, Gordon Byers, Lionel Van Praag

| 1933 | **BELLE VUE** | National League |

Frank Varey, Eric Langton, Bob Harrison, Eric Gregory, Max Grosskreutz, Bill Kitchen, Joe Abbott, Bronco Dixon, Frank Charles

| 1934 | **BELLE VUE** | National League |
| | Frank Varey, Eric Langton, Bill Kitchen, Frank Charles, Max Grosskreutz, Joe Abbott, Bob Harrison, Oliver Langton, Acorn Dobson | |

1934   **BELLE VUE**   National League
Frank Varey, Eric Langton, Bill Kitchen, Frank Charles, Max Grosskreutz, Joe Abbott, Bob Harrison, Oliver Langton, Acorn Dobson

1935   **BELLE VUE**   National League
Eric Langton, Frank Varey, Bill Kitchen, Joe Abbott, Max Grosskreutz, Bob Harrison, Oliver Langton, Eric Blain, Tommy Allott

1936   **BELLE VUE**   National League
Eric Langton, Frank Varey, Bill Kitchen, Max Grosskreutz, Bob Harrison, Joe Abbott, Wally Hull, Acorn Dobson, Oliver Langton

1937   **WEST HAM**   National League
Tiger Stevenson, Tommy Croombs, Bluey Wilkinson, Arthur Atkinson, Eric Chitty, Bronco Dixon, Phil Bishop, Charlie Spinks, Ken Brett

1938   **NEW CROSS**   National League
Stan Greatrex, Jack Milne, George Newton, Ron Johnson, Bill Longley, Joe Francis, Clem Mitchell, Goldy Restall, Ernie Evans

1946   **WEMBLEY**   National League
Bill Kitchen, Tommy Price, George Wilks, Bill Gilbert, Roy Craighead, Bob Wells, Alf Bottoms, Charlie May, Bronco Wilson

1947   **WEMBLEY**   National League
Bill Kitchen, Tommy Price, George Wilks, Bill Gilbert, Split Waterman, Roy Craighead, Bob Wells, Charlie May, Bronco Wilson

1948   **NEW CROSS**   National League
Ron Johnson, Eric French, Bill Longley, Jeff Lloyd, Geoff Pymar, Ray Moore, Frank Lawrence, Cyril Roger, George Newton

1949   **WEMBLEY**   National League
Bill Kitchen, Tommy Price, George Wilks, Split Waterman, Bill Gilbert, Fred Williams, Bob Wells, Bruce Abernethy, Alf Bottoms

1950   **WEMBLEY**   National League
Bill Kitchen, Tommy Price, Fred Williams, George Wilks, Bob Oakley, Bill Gilbert, Eric Williams, Bruce Abernethy, Bob Wells

1951   **WEMBLEY**   National League
Bill Kitchen, Tommy Price, Fred Williams, Bob Oakley, Bruce Abernethy, George Wilks, Jimmy Gooch, Eric Williams, Bob Wells

1952   **WEMBLEY**   National League
Bill Kitchen, Tommy Price, Fred Williams, Eric Williams, Trevor Redmond, Bob Oakley, George Wilks, Jimmy Gooch

1953   **WEMBLEY**   National League
Bill Kitchen, Tommy Price, Fred Williams, Eric Williams, Brian Crutcher, Eric French, Trevor Redmond, George Wilks, Jimmy Gooch

1954   **WIMBLEDON**   National League
Ronnie Moore, Geoff Mardon, Barry Briggs, Peter Moore, Cyril Brine, Olle Nygren, Don Perry, Cyril Maidment, Bill Longley, Reg Trott

136

| 1955 | **WIMBLEDON** | National League |
| | Ronnie Moore, Ron How, Barry Briggs, Peter Moore, Cyril Maidment, Alf Hagon, Cyril Brine, Reg Trott | |

1955   **WIMBLEDON**   National League
Ronnie Moore, Ron How, Barry Briggs, Peter Moore, Cyril Maidment, Alf Hagon, Cyril Brine, Reg Trott

1956   **WIMBLEDON**   National League
Ronnie Moore, Barry Briggs, Peter Moore, Ron How, Cyril Brine, Cyril Maidment, Alf Hagon, Bob Andrews, Gil Goldfinch

1957   **SWINDON**   National League
Ian Williams, Bob Roger, George White, Neil Street, Ken Middleditch, Mike Broadbanks, Ernie Lessiter, Al Sparrey

1958   **WIMBLEDON**   National League
Ronnie Moore, Barry Briggs, Ron How, Gerald Jackson, Cyril Maidment, Bob Andrews, Cyril Brine, Gerry King

1959   **WIMBLEDON**   National League
Ronnie Moore, Peter Moore, Ron How, Gerry Jackson, Cyril Maidment, Bob Andrews, Cyril Brine, Jim Tebby, Barry Briggs

1960   **WIMBLEDON**   National League
Ronnie Moore, Ron How, Bob Andrews, Cyril Brine, Cyril Maidment, Gerry Jackson, Jim Tebby, Gil Goldfinch, Ernie Baker

1961   **WIMBLEDON**   National League
Ronnie Moore, Bob Andrews, Ron How, Cyril Brine, Gerry Jackson, Gil Goldfinch, Jim Tebby, Cyril Maidment, Roy Trigg

1962   **SOUTHAMPTON**   National League
Dick Bradley, Barry Briggs, Bjorn Knutsson, Alby Golden, Cyril Roger, Peter Vandenberg, Reg Luckhurst, Brian Hanham

1963   **BELLE VUE**   National League
Peter Craven, Dick Fisher, Soren Sjosten, Gordon MacGregor, Cyril Maidment, Jim Yacoby, Bill Powell, Norman Nevitt

1964   **OXFORD**   National League
Jack Geran, Ron How, Arne Pander, Jimmy Gooch, Ronnie Genz, Colin Gooddy, John Bishop, Colin McKee, Eddie Reeves

1965   **WEST HAM**   British League
Ken McKinlay, Sverre Harrfeldt, Norman Hunter, Malcolm Simmons, Reg Trott, Brian Leonard, Ted Ede, Tony Clarke

1966   **HALIFAX**   British League
Eric Boothroyd, Eric Boocock, Dave Younghusband, Tommy Roper, Bert Kingston, Bob Jameson, Dennis Gavros, Greg Kentwell

1967   **SWINDON**   British League
Mike Broadbanks, Barry Briggs, Martin Ashby, Bob Kilby, Frank Shuter, Mike Keen, Peter Munday, Peter Jackson

1968   **COVENTRY**   British League
Ron Mountford, Nigel Boocock, Antonin Kasper, Col Cottrell, Roger Hill, Rick France, Tom Ridley, Les Owen, Chris Harrison

1969   **POOLE**   British League
Geoff Mudge, Pete Smith, Odd Fossengen, Bruce Cribb, Gordon Guasco, Frank Shuter, Ted Laessing, Mike Vernam, Ross Gilbertson

| 1970 | **BELLE VUE** Tommy Roper, Ivan Mauger, Soren Sjosten, Chris Pusey, Dave Hemus, Ken Eyre, Mike Hiftle, Eric Broadbelt, Steve Waplington | British League |

| 1971 | **BELLE VUE** Ivan Mauger, Soren Sjosten, Tommy Roper, Eric Broadbelt, Dave Hemus, Peter Collins, Chris Pusey, Ken Eyre, Alan Wilkinson | British League |

| 1972 | **BELLE VUE** Chris Pusey, Ivan Mauger, Soren Sjosten, Peter Collins, Eric Broadbelt, Alan Wilkinson, Ken Eyre, Paul Tyrer | British League |

| 1973 | **READING** Mick Bell, Anders Michanek, Dag Lovaas, Geoff Curtis, Richard May, Bernie Leigh, Jack Millen, Bobby McNeill | British League |

| 1974 | **EXETER** Ivan Mauger, Scott Autrey, Tony Lomas, Steve Reinke, Kevin Holden, Chris Julian, Frank Shuter, Mike Sampson, Peter Thompson | British League |

| 1975 | **IPSWICH** John Louis, Bill Sanders, Tony Davey, Mike Lanham, Mick Hines, Trevor Jones, Ted Howgego, Dave Gooderham | British League |

| 1976 | **IPSWICH** John Louis, Billy Sanders, Tony Davey, Mike Lanham, Ted Howgego, Dave Gooderham, Kevin Jolly, Trevor Jones, Andy Hines | British League |

| 1977 | **WHITE CITY** Gordon Kennett, Marek Cieslak, Steve Weatherley, Trevor Geer, Kai Niemi, Mike Sampson, Paul Gachet, Dave Kennett, Ian Clark, Brian Clark | British League |

| 1978 | **COVENTRY** Ole Olsen, Mitch Shirra, Alan Molyneux, Alf Busk, Jiri Stanci, Mick Bell, Gary Gugliemi, Frank Smith, Dave Mortiboys, Stuart Cope | British League |

Dick Case

Arthur Atkinson

Jack Ormston

Squib Burton

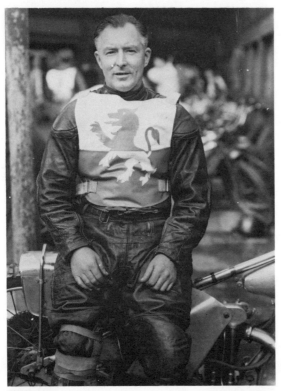

Bill Kitchen

Graham Warren

Ron Johnson

Wilbur Lamoreaux

140

Norman Parker

Alan Hunt

Jack Young

Brian Crutcher

141

Ovo Fundin

Barry Briggs

Nigel Boocock

Ronnie Moore

142

Anders Michanek

Ole Olsen

Malcolm Simmons

Ivan Mauger

One of Johnnie Hoskins' famous 'stunts' when he tried to introduce the first coloured rider to speedway. It proved to be a hoax! Rider on the right is Eric Chitty (Barratt's Photo Press)

Strange facts

There were a few pseudonyms used in the very early days but the strangest that I have ever come across was a gentleman calling himself L. Salmon Trout who rode at Bolton in 1928/29!

A rider called Godfrey Rabie from South Africa came over to ride at West Ham just before the war. Known as 'Scarface' he had some second-half rides at the Custom House track and at the end of an extremely short career, had torn down the fencing, broken both ankles, fractured his jaw, broken his nose and sustained a host of minor injuries!

On Easter Monday 1930, 71,311 people paid to go through the turnstiles of the Crystal Palace in Sydenham (London) during the day. Most of these lined up on the terraces to watch the speedway racing programme. Happy days!

A story to out do Johnnie Hoskins! Towards the end of a meeting at Wimbledon in 1931, a 'surprise item' took place in the form of a match race between a Chinese and an Australian aboriginal. The two riders concerned later turned out to be Frank Duckett and Mick Murphy in disguise. For the record, the 'Abo' won!

Notable firsts

During the first few months of Speedway Racing in England, the Australians were all-conquering. The first recorded instance of an Englishman beating an Australian was when Roger Frogley defeated Charlie Datson in a match race in 1928.

The first recorded dead-heat in a league match was between Norman Burton of Birmingham and Harringay's Ray Parsons, who tied for second place at Perry Barr in May 1929.

In recent years there have been many appeals by teams when the decision has gone against them and as a result, we have sometimes seen league tables adjusted after the end of the season. The first match to be re-run following a protest, was between Perry Barr (Birmingham) and White City (London) in August 1929. The Brummie side had lost by three points but protested because White City did not field a complete team and had to make impromptu arrangements. The appeal was successful and the match re-run later in the season.

The first league match to take place was between Southampton and Birmingham's other side, Hall Green, in 1929.

It is believed that the first rider to score maximum points from three completed rides was England and Stamford Bridge rider, Gus Kuhn.

An unpleasant first this – the first rider to be killed on the track as far as we can tell, was Charles Biddle who was involved in a crash at Stamford Bridge in May 1928. He died in hospital six days later.

The first regulations for the conduct of motorcycle competitions on tracks, were prepared in the early part of 1929 by the A-CU Sub-Committee of the Track Licensing Committee consisting of the following members: G.R. Allan (Chairman), Cecil Smith, R.M. Samuel and T.W. Loughborough (Secretary A-CU).

We see a number of budding young riders these days, scorching round before the meetings commence, on specially built miniature bikes. The first mascot to give exhibitions was seven-year-old 'Hurricane' Chambers who performed at Harringay, Wimbledon and White City tracks in 1929.

The winner of the very first race in the original Southern League in 1929 was Cyril Taft.

The first member of the English Royal Family to visit Speedway was HRH Prince George, father of the present Duke of Kent, who turned up at London's White City Stadium in 1929.

A first of some renown. At the original High Beech meeting in February 1928, the opening race was won by a novice motor cyclist named A. Barker, who thus unknowingly carved for himself a special place in the annals of speedway racing.

The Veteran Dirt Track Riders Association

There has been a lot of interest recently, centred on the activities and make-up of the VDTRA. I therefore asked Jack Barnett the ever-popular Secretary, to tell a little of its origin and its aims.

'When Peter Arnold, an enthusiastic speedway supporter, announcer and writer for motorcycle and speedway magazines heard that Lord Montagu was preparing to open a Speedway Museum, he acquired lists of former riders from various sources and then set about tracing their whereabouts. How he managed this I just do not know, but I received a 'phone call one day saying that there would be a gathering of pioneer riders at Lord Montagu's place near Beaulieu and would I like to go? Yes, was the answer to that and I received an invitation from Beaulieu saying that the Speedway Section of the Museum would be opened on Sunday, 12th May 1957 and would I attend and take tea afterwards with his Lordship. That was indeed a memorable Sunday – there must have been at least 50 former riders present and my wife's tale is that there were these fat, bald headed old gentlemen looking at each other and shouting "No it can't be" and the reply "Yes it is, how are you?".

Some 1929 Douglases miraculously appeared and Phil Bishop, having got astride one, proceeded to tear up Lord Montagu's favourite flower beds with gay abandon and from that get-together the Association was born. On 26th April 1958, we had our first Dinner at the Royal Forest Hotel at Chingford, not far from High Beech, honoured by the presence of Lord Sempill and with a very full attendance. Since then there has been an annual Dinner/Dance with the support seeming to grow year by year.

The original name of the "Club" was the Pioneer Dirt Track Riders' Association but it was realised that the Pioneers would not last for ever (!) so it was changed to the Veteran Dirt Track Riders' Association and has gone from strength to strength ever since. Then came 1968 and the 40th Anniversary of the first dirt track meeting. Peter arranged a gathering at High Beech which was attended by supporters' clubs from tracks all over the country and by a large contingent of riders – a terrific success.

However, in September 1969, Peter, sadly, died of a heart attack – this was within only a week or so of the Annual General Meeting which was held as planned and the job voted to me. As mentioned earlier, the main event of the year is the Dinner/Dance and 1978 saw our 21st. Membership is increasing each year and we now have well over 200 members including many from Australia, South Africa and the USA. New members are always welcome and the qualification is to have ridden on a track at least 20 years ago and the objects of the Association are purely social or benevolent in character.'

Keen supporters and particularly the older ones may be interested in the following list of past Presidents of the Association: Mart Seiffert, Frank Varey, Gus Kuhn, Phil Bishop, Jack Barnett, George Greenwood, Wal Phillips, Squib Burton, Bill Kitchen, Harry Taft, Jack Parker, Johnnie Hoskins, Claude Rye, Syd Edmonds, Westy Westwood, Tiger Hart, Bill Pitcher and this year's President, Morian Hansen.

At a VDTRA dinner. Johnnie Hoskins appears to be enjoying himself (A.C. Weedon)

Lord Montagu talks to a group of Southampton riders at Beaulieu on the occasion of the official opening of the Beaulieu Speedway Museum

Bill Pitcher of Harringay and Belle Vue fame, VDTRA President in
the Golden Jubilee year

Morian Hansen, the first of the great Danes, President of the VDTRA
in 1979

149

Three top notch ex dons

Ray Tauser – American ace

150

Legendary Australian Skipper, Vic Huxley, with his famous pet terrier mascot (Fox Photos)

Claude Rye

The Brothers

Ray and Vic Duggan

Jack Parker with brother Norman

Bert and Cyril Roger

Conclusion

It is 50 years since League racing was introduced, a move which began to transform racing in this country. During that first season, racing was perhaps a little primitive, but then riders began to buckle down to learn their trade seriously. The sport became more competitive and more sophisticated. Styles and conditions started to change. Men who had ruled the roost in individual combat learned, and then perfected, the art of team riding which, with notable exceptions, has to a great extent been allowed to fall into decay. Ronnie Moore was one of the last of the really great team riders, men who could shepherd home partners much slower than themselves or the opposition. Significantly, he was trained by Norman Parker, himself one of the game's supreme artists in this aspect of racing. By 1937/38, riders had become fully skilled; they could almost all be identified by their individual styles and I think that this period could justifiably be called speedway's Golden Age. There does appear to be a widespread belief today, that comparatively speaking, racing during the first ten years was conducted at a snail's pace. Those holding this view would do well to ponder on the fact that even in the early thirties, Tom Farndon and Arthur Jervis were putting up speeds of 50 mph over four laps at Crystal Palace and Leicester, respectively.

I am sometimes asked how the stars of yesteryear would fare against today's big names. It is my view that the Huxleys, Farndons, Parkers, Milnes etc., were real champions and would have remained champions on today's equipment and track surfaces. Similarly, although many of today's 'stars' would have floundered on the deep cinders and differently prepared tracks of yesteryear, the Maugers, Collins and Olsens would still have reached the top of their profession.

During the developing years, England took over as the principal speedway nation, and on the International scene at the time of writing, England looks set to reign for some years, with their crop of fine young riders. True, the home country lost a rather strange series last year to the combined strength of Australia and New Zealand, followed by the totally unexpected defeat at the hands of the Olsen-inspired Denmark in the four-man World Cup Team event on a German track, but how the Danes would fare in a full six or eight-man team international is problematical — perhaps we shall get a chance to judge quite soon. The outlook seems bleak for Sweden, who lost in Tommy Jansson, the one man who looked set to follow in the footsteps of Fundin, Knutsson, Nygren and Co. Poland's position is little better and Russia have seemingly nothing to offer at present. Can New Zealand find another two or three in the mould of Mauger, Briggs and Moore? Will Finland produce a few others with the tremendous potential of Ila Teromaa?

However, conditions change quite quickly in this sport of ours — look how Sweden slumped from glory in 1970 to almost complete ignominy a few short years later. It is an interesting situation. The sport has always managed to supply its quota of shocks and we can look forward with anticipation to many more intriguing international and domestic track battles. With 90,000 people at last season's Wembley World Final, the outlook in England cannot be bad.

Best of British

Tom Farndon. National Speedway Champion and British Individual Champion (T.H. Everitt)

Frank Charles. National Speedway Champion

Eric Langton. National Speedway Champion

155

Jack Parker. National Speedway Champion, Speedway Riders Champion and Match Race Champion (Lewis W. Gale)

Fred Williams. World Champion

Peter Collins. World Champion

Tommy Price. World Champion and British Riders Champion

Peter Craven. World Champion

Action through the decades

Action from the 20's. Vic Huxley and George Reynard in 1929 at Halifax (C.A. Shore)

Action from the 30's. A race in progress at the pre-war 'Amateur' circuit at Norwich c.1937.

Action from the late 40's. Stan Williams of
Sheffield holds the inside with partner
Tommy Bateman alongside and Gruff
Garland of Ashfield trying an outside sweep
(Sheffield Telegraph)

Action from the 50's. New Cross Skipper,
Eric French tries to force his way through
Bradford riders Alex Burrow and Arthur
Bush at Odsel in 1951 (J.S. Grace)

162

Action from the 60's. The champions clash.
Ove Fundin (left) tries to overtake Bjorn
Knutsson

Heat 5 gets under way during the Blue Riband meeting at Poole Speedway on August 14th 1974. The riders are left to right: John Louis, Antoni Woryna, Dave Jessup and Martin Ashby (Cecil Bailey)